The Invisible Real Fathers Guide

A Guide For Men Whom Are Or Wish To Be Real Fathers

Derek McNeil

Order this book online at www.trafford.com
or email orders@trafford.com

Most Trafford titles are also available at major online book retailers.

Art work By Derek McNeil.

Printed in the United States of America.

ISBN: 978-1-4669-8343-4 (sc)
ISBN: 978-1-4669-8344-1 (e)

Trafford rev. 03/28/2013

 www.trafford.com

North America & international
toll-free: 1 888 232 4444 (USA & Canada)
phone: 250 383 6864 ♦ fax: 812 355 4082

Table of Contents

Dedication

This book is in dedication to all fathers and potential fathers out there whom are doing their very best to care for and take care of their children no matter the sacrifice they may have to give regardless of whether they are doing so with or without a spouse. I applaud each and every one of you not just from me but from the creator of us all whom imbues us with the strength to know and do that which we know is right despite the negative stereotypes ascribed to us by various sources in our society and the negative examples shown of us again and again with little regard to those of us whom fly in the face of such.

Special Thanks

I would like to give special thanks to the Creator of us all and all whom have given me the inspiration and proper nudge to write and publish this book from the idea and entire template of this book residing in my mind. I would like to also give my thanks and appreciation to all who gave me the courage to push on and do what was necessary that this book would become a reality rather than a lost entity residing in the depths of my mind, chained to my own fears as to whether or not anyone would be interested in that which I would bring forth and have to say. How much is there that is worthwhile that never reaches the light of day for fear of what others will think and or say languishing in noble minds?

Important Notice to The Reader

No responsibility is assumed on the part of the author, publishers or distributors of this book should you choose to use the information in this book. I only profess to be a father whom all his life has been doing the best he can imbued with a strong desire to help others with a major subject that is not taught. I am not advocating a role reversal for men and women nor am I writing this to deride neither the opposite sex nor anyone else for that matter. Only a guide for men whom desire to do all they can for their families or families to be and men whom find themselves in the situation where everything and all responsibility falls upon them for whatever reasons those may be. Parenthood is an art that should be shared by a man and a woman; however, it doesn't always work out that way for whatever reasons those may be.

As for my qualifications to write this book, they are derived from my ongoing experience being a 100% real father to children whom I love very much and are in my care. It has come hard but yet it has had its joyous moments as well.

Preface

Why this book? Because I believe it is truly needed. Yes, the traditional role has been for men to be just breadwinners. But what happens if you have to be the breadwinner and the caregiver at the same time because your significant other can no longer do it, is no longer there to do it or will no longer and just plain outright won't do it? What if she was never the mothering type to begin with or you've discovered she is such you wouldn't trust her to take care of even a gerbil? Well that just leaves you, unless you are planning to dump your children upon your folks, the system or who ever. I hope that's not you, but then if it was, you would not be reading this. So far as I can see no real effort has been made to give men, young men, any kind of guidance to be really good fathers. You can be a tough manly man and still be a good father. There are plenty of help aides for women but you just don't see this for men. In this book I am attempting to provide such based on my own real life experiences and what I have done with my own children in my care. I may not be able to cover everything, but I will do my best to come as close as reasonably possible. Whether you have made the choice or you have been surprised and discovered the choice has chosen you, I will do my best to give you the information that may help you do the best job possible and hopefully also save you some pain as well. Some things I say in this book may not seem to apply to fatherhood at first, but believe me it does as it is interrelated. Nothing happens in a vacuum. There is a reason for everything and many things that don't seem related actually are thus having an effect on other things. So it is with everything I touch upon in this book.

Introduction

Why did I say the Invisible Real Fathers? First of all, it takes more than bringing a child into the world to be a father because anybody can be a sperm donor. Secondly, being a real father is just as tough and demanding as being a good mother. Finally, real fathers who are out there taking care of and doing for their children receive very little or no credit as though we do not exist. As a matter of fact, it seems to be understood that we do not.

So what is the definition of a real father? Is it pollinating some pretty flower and then marveling at the seed you just created and having nothing else to do with that seed except going to work to provide the basic needs for that seed and sometimes not even that? Is it producing a whole bunch of those seeds like trophies on a wall? Is it doing something like mentioned in the past couple of questions and then spending just a little time with those seeds at the game later when they are old enough, stuff like that but not much else? Hummm. If you look in the dictionary, the definition for father minus the religious definitions is as follows: 1. A male parent. 2. One deserving the respect and love given to a father. 3. To treat or care for as a father. Now if you read the definition for mother from the same dictionary you get: 1. A female parent. 2. To give birth to; also: PRODUCE 3. To care for or protect like a mother. These are nice definitions but according to society norms I thought the man was suppose to do the protecting. For all intensive purposes it would appear men have been relegated to the posthumous role of mere sperm donor. I think men need a new definition for father. Anyone reading this may have his or her own variation but I think it should be: I. A male parent. 2. One deserving the respect love and honor entitled them for being a good caring father who raises their children as well as provides for them 3. The co producer of child or children with a female parent. 4. The male father figure whom cares for and protects their family and offspring in their care as well as teacher and imparter of wisdom that only a father can do. Likewise, the definition of mother needs to be similarly overhauled.

Why do I say this? Because families in America are falling apart and what a mother and father are supposed to be have been seriously disfigured and in the case of fathers mauled. It would seem that fathers are considered non-entities, non-necessary, non-important, non-good, etc. etc. Neither men nor women are really being taught what a mother or father is supposed to be. Wait, yes they are. They are being taught by what they see in the media whether it is movies; TV, TV talk shows and those images are not too good. According to what we see and hear via the media, mothers are supposed to be the sole caretakers because the man cannot be relied upon to be there. Men are nothing but sperm donors whom are only good for child support. That was crude but that seems to be the general message as positive images for fathers are in very short supply while women are put on a pedestal with the twist of being victims of men. That's actually an ugly image for the women because why would you want to be a victim no matter how high the pedestal? As a matter of fact, women have the idea that everything is the man's fault without ever looking in the mirror at their own actions. It seems to be a rare woman whom will take responsibility for what she herself does. These images teach our youth what to expect to be and be. We need new images and we need them now as the moral fabric of the US is falling apart and the backbone of the US is the family. I am just making a point.

The purpose of this book though is to give support to and act as a guide to the men whom want to be and or are real fathers. I'm talking about all men whom have wanted to escape the stereotypes I just mentioned. The fathers who are truly there for their families and in some cases that just means the children. Contrary to popular opinion, there are plenty of deadbeat moms out there too. You don't have to be devoid of your children to be a deadbeat parent. It is not as pronounced with women as they are automatically labeled as being the better parent and usually given the children. They have the benefit of support organizations and group's men simply do not have. There is always someone available to help women in some form or fashion. Men do not have such an infrastructure in place for them. They must at all times be their own infrastructure. It would be great if the infrastructure in place also responded to good fathers but such is non-existent. Contrary to popular belief there are many men whom would or do gladly take the responsibility of raising their children and they do so with or without a spouse. If we fathers are lucky we have the help of the children's grandparents.

I know I will catch some flak for that remark, but how many of us know of women who have custody of the children whom spend all kinds of money on their nails, clothes for themselves, etc. while the kids are in need of shoes, clothes, going to the dentist, etc. Just because you have custody doesn't make you an automatic great parent. To that end, there are a lot of fathers out there whom do everything a woman does and sometimes then some to take care of their children but you don't hear much about them or nothing at all hence the reason in the title I said "Invisible Real Fathers". We are for all intensive purposes invisible, don't exist, whatever. There are many of you whom when the teacher first meets you and finds you are the one doing everything, she gives you an astonished incredulous look like she just can't believe it. You will hear, "Where is the mother", like it's a broken record. If you are like me, you have been taking care of your children and know what all women whom are good mothers go through to take care of their children and you take it in stride. By the way, you don't have to be divorced, separated or whatever to be a single parent. Whether man or woman, you can be married and still be a single parent if you are the one whom does everything. This is an unacknowledged fact. Notice, I did not discriminate. I want to make it clear right now this is not a women bashing book, although men have had to suffer a lot of bashing by all forms of media thanks to the rotten apples that are in every group that may be discussed. It seems to be easier and more exciting to talk of those whom do bad than those whom do good. The bashing has to stop somewhere though. Real men, real fathers, you know who you are, be proud. This book is dedicated to you.

Pre-Chapter
List of Things Every Good Father Should Have

1. Expansive Tool Kit—Real men have tools. Your tool kit should include: screw drivers, (can be bought in kits), wrenches, (you want to have several different types like the ones that self adjust for instance), various types of screws, nuts and bolts, nails, at least one drill and a dremel tool or two, (a good dremel tool decked out with all the bits can really be a man's best friend), a socket set, rulers of various lengths, electrical tape, balance, hammer, chisel, saw, etc. Why do you want all of this? Because you can repair furniture with it, hang new blinds with it, fix, modify, and up-grade any number of things with it. Work on your car. Repair a desk, chairs or table. It can be a lifesaver literally. You'd be surprised what uses you will find for it especially with a child or children around. Children can be destructive. Your child might damage something you can't buy anymore or will cost a lot for you to replace or hire someone to fix. That tool kit may be your rescue agent.

2. Sewing kit—You never know when you will need one of these. It could make the difference between buying a new coat, chair, couch, belt, etc, and repairing it like or very close to new. It can be used to refurbish things if you are creative and of course put a button back on your or your child's pants, shirt, coat, etc too.

3. A really good juicer and food processor. I'll elaborate more on that later.

4. A good weight set and weight bench. Keep in shape. You will need to be able to keep up with your children and in the case of boys; you may have one whom

will constantly seek to out do you so you better be two steps ahead of him and in some cases her. You never ever want your children to get the idea they can beat you, as that is often the end of respect for you, not to mention loss of disciplinary control. Besides keeping in shape, working out can be a good stress reducer.

5. A really good cleaning kit and carpet steam cleaner that can also clean furniture. Babies have accidents often in places you really would hate them to, like on your cloth couch and or in your favorite chair, and children in general can be messy and undo your day by eating or doing things where you told them not to and then making a mess showing why you told them not to in the first place. You'd better be prepared to be able to clean up these miss-haps or you will find yourself in a rather unsanitary nasty looking home. Think of the people you know with children and you walked into their home and wondered what in the world happened to their carpet and furniture and what in the world were those spots and dark gray things in their carpet. Besides, if you can't keep a clean home, you will find it a magnet for various things that love those kinds of surroundings. Think roaches, lice, mites, mice, etc, etc.

6. A really good computer, better if you know how to build your own. You should have one for you, and one for your children.

7. A really good camera that you can hook up to your computer. You never know when a precious moment will come along that you will want to capture for all time. Your children are children only once.

8. A really good family doctor you can trust.

9. A really good first aid kit. You never know when you may need one, especially with children whom can be rough and like to explore various places you may not wish them to.

10. Several salvage bins. What do I mean by that?
    When something breaks, don't immediately throw it away. Salvage what you can from it. Your child's toy or whatever breaks, salvage the screws and

anything else that may be useful from it. Salvaged buttons can go into your sewing kit, screws into your tool kit, etc. However, if your vacuum cleaner breaks and can't be repaired or it's just time to replace it, get the belts out of it and other things that can be useful. You may need it for your next vacuum cleaner and buying belts for a vacuum cleaner can be an exercise in frustration. That's just an example. You will need something to place salvaged materials in. Don't be a literal pack rat and make your place junky but salvaged materials can be a lifesaver.

11. A damn good washer and dryer. You don't have to be extravagant but don't be cheap either. Cheap washing machines and dryers can be frustrating as they usually don't get the job done so do not skimp in this area. If you can get a good set cheap that does the job well great but otherwise look at quality first then worry about the price.

12. Keep a landline. Yes, I know everyone is trying to just have a mobile phone these days, but just because everybody else seems to be doing something does not make it the thing to do. You should only use mobile phones away from home. When you are home use a landline only. The reason. All mobile phones produce radiation. Its low level radiation but it is still there and damaging. A slow poison if you will. A slow poison may not get you as fast as something quick like a gun but in the end, it will still get you. Low-level radiation is even more dangerous to children than it is to you as their bodies and brains are still growing and developing. There is a host of information on this subject you should look up. The phone companies are interested in you going mobile as it saves them money. They could care less about your health.

13. File Cabinet. You need this to file not only your important documents, but your children's documents as well. A file just for medical information, school information, and birth records, etc.

14. Some place you can go and be left alone. You must have some place you can go and be left alone in peace from time to time. It will keep you sane and keep your stress levels in check. Every parent needs this. You will need it to have some time to collect your thoughts and get a break, whether from your

children, work or your spouse. It can be as simple as having a room you can retreat to and no one is allowed to come in and bother you, but you must have it. If you can't get such peace at home then you will have to go to the park or something of the sort with the key word alone, no one else, so that you can relax. This is not to be a cover to be with someone else.

15. Two nice big dictionaries and thesauruses. One for you and one for your children. That way, if and when they take the dictionary designated for them for granted and it starts falling apart, you will have a nice good one for you. Do not allow them to use that which is for you unless you want it torn up too.

16. When old enough a good encyclopedia set. Get both, the good old fashion books and the DVD variety that you can use on the computer. Why both? What do you do if the computer goes down at the most inopportune time? If you have the old fashion encyclopedia set continue on. If you don't, you will wish you did and hope that the nearest library is still open and accessible.

17. Heavy duty dose of faith in the Creator that they can weather whatever their family i.e. children, significant other and quite possibly other family members may put in their way of ultimately doing the best job possible steering and raising a family as the Creator intended.

18. Given the increase in disasters, I would highly recommend putting together some kind of survival and first aid kit. I'd include rope, implements for setting fires, medicine, water treatment and even a supply of seeds. Learn to use not only a gun but even a bow and arrow. No, I'm not crazy but hurricanes Katrina, Ike and the earthquakes that have struck Haiti and Chili have made an impression upon me. Here in the United States we have the Yellow Stone super volcano and also a major Thrust Fault in the mid and mid northern United States. Sometime soon they are going to go off. We also do not know what will happen regarding climate change. We may actually go through another little ice age as a result. We should all have on our minds what we are going to do as if catastrophe happens there may be no help coming. By the way, if you decide to keep a store of seeds, make damn sure they are not GMO but are instead verifiably organic. GMO seed suppliers want you to keep coming back to them

for more seed. That's a very bad thing if you can't still do that right. Hence, make sure you have seeds that will allow you to cultivate your own seeds. I could keep adding to this list if I really think about it but I think this covers the basics. Adding to this list from this point depends on your situation and home environment, which of course is different for everyone. Add to this list as you see fit.

From Small to Big

Everything starts small before it can be big and so shall it be with you and your family.

So start well.

For how you **start** shall play a major role in **determining** how your budding family finishes.

All things start this way, whether they are bad or good, they start small.

So take care and start good for the alternative will be *very* bad for you and those you love who shall start small.

Notes

Chapter One
So You Want To Be A Real Father One Day.
Where Do You Start?

You start by making sure that first you are really ready which means more than being ready in heart and mind although those are equally as important. You must be financially stable and that means more than just having a job. I'm going to tell you what I was never told as there was no one around who knew better to tell me and you may probably have experienced the same issue as your parents can not tell you what they themselves do not know and were not taught.

1. If you are unmarried and have no children now nor any on the way, do not rush nor put yourself in a position for it to happen. Even if you have someone you think you really love hold your horses. Instead, prepare. What do I mean? What is being prepared? Usually you are told to just get a good job but is that really enough? NO!! It's not! Even if you think back before the economic hard times of now, (an understatement), it wasn't. What if you have children, bought a home, car, and then lose your job. What now? The bills don't go away and mouths have to be fed. Even if you don't lose your job, with both you and your spouse working, where is the time to properly raise the children? Traditionally, jobs have had consideration for women regarding children ranging from good to poor but for men it is so non-existent as to be rated as negative consideration, which is absolutely awful if you are a single father. That means whether you are a man or a woman, you must give consideration to children long before they are here. Once they are here it is too late as children are not

commodities. They are neither toys nor pets. They need large quantities of love and care to become well-rounded positive contributors to society and to carry on your family legacy in a positive way. If they don't get that you may have just birthed a burden to society mildly or horrendously speaking. You see, you have to be at work at a certain time and you get off at a certain time. Children don't conform to your schedule though. As babies they come with ever changing schedules. Those schedules change again when they are tots. Then again when they are school age all the way up to high school. Someone has to be there for them through all of that. The time must come from somewhere and if you don't have the time there are others you may not like that will. That could be their peers whom don't know squat themselves or someone from the street whom you really don't want fooling with them and contrary to the media and popular belief, the street is the street whether you're in an undesirable neighborhood or suburbia. Negative characters that want to misguide and use your children may come in different forms but they are everywhere no matter where you are and they are waiting. So before you do any pollinating, this must be thought out and planned for no one else is going to care and do it for you.

2. So what do you need past just employment? You need to look at a job as a means to an end instead of a solution. What do I mean by that? You may have gone to college and got a great job but eventually all jobs come to an end and that doesn't necessarily mean retirement. So what you need to do with your job is live off only what you need and find a means to invest the rest, in mutual funds for instance and establish a retirement plan. Also, purchase some life insurance, preferably term life. You will get it at a low price while you are young and will have it paid up when you are old. Don't blow it on that hopped up car you always wanted. That can come later. Don't go out and prematurely buy your dream home. That too can come later when the time is right, besides, a 30-40 year home loan is more like financial herpes rather than buying a home free and clear, but I digress. By the way, buy a home in your name only before you get married and put it in a land trust. Doing this may save you some pain later. You will have to decide what to invest in, as there is no silver bullet and what works for one may not necessarily work for someone else. But, that investment

must be something that will give you a stable return. In other words, something that will provide you with money in the event you lose your job. Something that maybe will ultimately make it so you don't need a job as like I said, you don't want to be in a position where losing your job means you lose everything. I found that lesson out the hard way. You have to understand, family may be there to help or they may not. In fact, even if they can they are not obligated to and may not. Don't put yourself in that position. As a nation we are littered with families now in that position and as a whole, we are suffering for it but once again, I digress. So to recap, before you get hitched and combine genes, save up your money to create a nest egg that you don't touch unless its an emergency, keep clean credit, make financial goals and put a committed plan into action for not just financial stability but also independence and have it bear fruit before you do anything else. After you get hitched and children are on the way it's too late. The demands and new responsibilities are going to slam into you. I'm not saying it's insurmountable but you may find it like mission impossible as you are pulled in all kinds of different directions by all of your new responsibilities. And if that pretty little flower you pollinated is not in your corner and on the same wavelength as you, you could be facing mission impossible because if she is not working in harmony with you then she's working against you. Period. This leads me to number three.

3. Choose carefully the flower you want to pollinate. The most beautiful rose has painful thorns when you embrace it. So pick a flower that has no thorns or at the very least as few of them as possible. This topic could be a book unto itself given what I've learned about it the hard way but you must choose your woman whom will be the bearer of your offspring very carefully. I guarantee you she's choosing you as carefully as she can so you should be doing some careful choosing as well. I could write a book for the women too as they seem to have rather off qualifications for choosing a man just as we seem to have a lack of good qualifications for choosing good women. If it wasn't so, why is the status of relationships in America so screwed up? To that end, be sure and inquire with any potential mate when appropriate about any illnesses and or genetic

diseases that may run in the family. If such is found you have to ask yourself do you want your potential offspring to have such?

4. If a good woman is what you want, the first question you better ask yourself is "If I was a baby yet to be born, is this whom I'd want to be my mother?" If the answer is no, whatever you do, get away from that woman. Let her go. The earth can shake, sparks may fly, the angels may sing and or stuff may taste like the sweetest candy chardonnay. Get over it because clouded judgment resulting from a few moments of pleasure can be the beginning of suffering for a very long time. Let her go if there are nagging doubts particularly if you find yourself constantly wondering, "If she's like this now what will she be like if I marry her?" If you get her pregnant it's over and you're stuck one way or another. You can't run. Remember, you're a good man so there's no escape once that happens, (at least not for a while), so avoid all such women. I'm not saying get an ugly woman. You must be attracted to her. I'm just saying that looks and ability to achieve materially can't be the main qualification. Who you choose must have demonstrated good moral character and be a good mother type. She must be in your corner and supportive of you and you in kind to her. I must add she should be able to be a good provider in the case something happens to you. She should be comfortably attractive and lastly but extremely important, the two of you must be able to be comfortable with each other and get along no matter how bad life is. She must be peaceful and enjoy being and having a peaceful home with you. Not silent nor a wallflower but peaceful. If any of these are missing you are going to have problems. By comfortable with each other I mean you must be able to be yourselves around each other in totality. You must be able to be honest with each other at all times without repercussions. You must be able to tell her things without worrying if she is going to use what you say against you later. And she should be able to expect the same from you too. You must be able to come home and have peace and not worry about what it's going to be this time when you walk through the door. If not, your union is a time bomb and your offspring will suffer as a result in the process. Remember, you have to be a good father so if things go south you can't just think about what is good for you and leave as that

may run contrary to any children you may have had. Part of protecting your children is to make sure you don't put them in a position you will regret and one day must apologize to them for later. You can never make up such errors. There is no do over button. There are those of you whom may be reading this whom already knows exactly what I'm talking about and it really hurts when a child asks, "Dad, why did you choose momma, she's—you insert the various descriptive adjectives that may be used and appropriate."

Plan how you are going to raise your children before they are even conceived. This can be controversial. If you are a vegetarian you better get a vegetarian woman and vice versa for women to. If you are neat and you want your children to be neat choose someone whom is neat without getting a neat freak which can be almost as bad as getting a slob. If you want your children to be organized and prompt don't choose Ms. Slow I will get up when I feel like it. If you want your children to be smart quick thinkers that excel you better not get a space cadet no matter how good she looks and how far in space she can take you if you know what I mean. If you want your children breast fed, (this should not be an option. All children should be breast fed; preferably for 3 years no less than 1), you better make sure your potential mate feels the same way or you just got yourself a fight. Be sure your potential mate is on the same page with you about how the children will be raised, period, without waver. You have to understand, you will not be the only influence on any children you have with the woman you choose. So will she. A child is a genetic and spiritual combination of the parents. Even though a woman carries the child in her womb, half of that child is you and half is her. Period. She didn't have the child on her own. Even if a woman goes to a sperm bank and gets the sperm and impregnates herself, the child is still half her and half the genetic spiritual make up of whomever the sperm donor is present or not. Period. The contribution of fathers to the making of children is very underrated and berated so any women whom may read this you better keep this in mind too. Don't let a fool be the contributor to the other half of what makes up your child! Once the child is born, you do not know what characteristics the child will end up with. You don't know which will be dominant and which will be recessive. You could be Mr. Neat but Ms

Junkie's junkie gene may dominate the child. You could be Mr. Early, but Ms Late's late gene dominates. You could be Mr. Clean but Ms Nasty's nasty gene dominates. You get my drift. The child could have a whole bunch of your good characteristics early on as a child but then, as they get older, the bad characteristics of the other suddenly takes over and shuts off the good ones the child got from you. Now what you have is a struggle because you just got a new job with your child. Find a way to turn off those bad characteristics and turn back on the good ones you know the child has. You may only be partially successful or fail completely but for the sake of the child you must try. Guess what, this is super stressful and can give you gray hairs and possibly other health problems. Parenting is hard enough as it is without making things harder by making mistakes that could have been avoided. You must understand me. No one is perfect and there is no perfect mate. But you better get as damn close as you possibly can within reason because if you choose badly, guess what you can expect from trying to raise the children with this person. Once again, in the name of fairness, for any one woman reading this reverse it upon yourself for the same information applies. A really good book needs to be devoted to the subject of male/female relations in a way that probably hasn't been done before. Be sure and choose a healthy mate and get your own health in order.

5. If you are a junk food junkie go to junk food junkies anonymous or something. If you are an alcoholic go to alcoholics anonymous. If you are on drugs go to . . . . You get my drift. Do not, I repeat, do not have children if you have such problems. Get help, get off the stuff and wait a minimum of 3 years in the case of all drugs, (that includes alcohol), to get it out of your system with the help of someone whom knows how to safely clean toxins out of the body. You don't want this crap going into the seed that will produce your offspring whether you are a man or woman. If you know you have bad habits do something about them now before ever considering having a child. If not, they will become apart of the unborn child. You must care and love yourself enough that you don't do this to the child and the supposedly other parent. Remember, the child is born innocent and you are in the wrong if you impose such things on

the child for they have no choice in the matter and did not ask to be here. Please develop good healthy eating habits long before conception. I'm not telling you to be a vegetarian, (but it sure helps being at least close to that ideal), but you must seek to have a consistent good diet that includes as much healthy diversity as possible devoid of toxic foods. Eliminate white flour and refined sugar products from the diet for instance. Have a diet that includes a diversity of vegetables instead of a typical mono-diet. Stay away from foods that have preservatives and other chemicals that do your body no good. Try to eat organic and as naturally as possible. If you don't know how to cook learn now. It's not only important what you put into yourself but what you put in your child as well. I will give more on this later. So in closing on this section, prepare, choose well, care for and love yourself before you choose someone to love and care for and then produce others with them whom you absolutely unequivocally must love, care and provide for no matter if it is together with a spouse or alone without a spouse. By the way, you can be married and still alone without a spouse. That goes for both, men and women.

Notes

Chapter Two
Childcare Before Conception

O k, you've chosen a mate or she chose you and she's great. You've avoided getting her pregnant before marriage. You've got your plans in effect and everything is going great.

Your woman is committed to your plans and will not be a hindrance to you nor your future children and to be fair you are no hindrance to her and you both know and have agreed on your roles. You have both together and I repeat, both together decided the time is right. Don't pollinate her just yet. As a matter of fact, it would be a good idea to wait 3 to 4 years before getting your spouse pregnant. That will give you both time to make sure your union will be long lasting and work not to mention not getting children involved in the middle if it won't. During that timeframe, although both of you have a health plan in effect and are both working out and are healthy, you should clean your bodies out before the conception of a child. Remember I mentioned using the services of a natural professional that knows how to safely clean out the body. Well it's time to get with such a person and clean out you and your woman. You want to do this so that conception can be as non toxic as possible. You want you and your woman to be as free of the toxins that naturally accumulate in the body as possible. This will produce higher quality sperm in you and eggs in her. Also, do a spiritual purge on yourselves as well. That does not mean become religious fanatics. Get all of the negativity out of your environment as much as you can. The less stress you are both under the better and I don't mean just for this period. Whatever is happening to the two of you spiritually whether positive or negative, it will go into the child at conception, during gestation, labor, birth and all during rearing. Trust me, it has an effect.

Now, from the moment you start this, don't have sex for 3 months. You read me right. Don't have sex. No I'm not crazy. I love to wreck beds just like the next guy. By not having sex, not only will the sperm reserve be replenished, but it also gets a rest. The same happens for the woman. Both of your reproductive systems get a rest. Minerals get replenished. It will be hard but worth it. After the 3 months is up choose a day that neither one of you have to go anywhere nor will be disturbed. Massage each other from head to toe and tell one another how much you love each other during the process and truly mean it. Please give her just as good a message as she gave you and vice versa. Transition to love making and make sure when you get through she knows how much you love her. You just accomplished something special besides possible conception. The lovemaking was special after a 3-month hiatus, the quality of the lovemaking was high and thus so should your seed have been and lastly, a spiritual connection you will both appreciate if it wasn't already there and made stronger. By the way, during loving making be very sure to give praise to the creator and ask the creator for the child that you want. Be specific to as the creator can have a sense of humor you may not appreciate. Repeat this until you know conception has occurred.

Now for the part that will probably make you angry with me. Once your woman is pregnant, don't make love to her until after the child is born. Yea, I know you want to curse me out and with hormones raging she probably will want to curse you out. However, it will be good for the unborn child. When a woman is pregnant, her body throws itself into gear to have the child. That means hormonal changes as well as physical ones. Whatever hormones are in her blood will be shared with the unborn child just as food will. Whatever she feels spiritually so too will be shared with the unborn child. So keep it clean. Keep the hormones and spirit of production, (you know what I mean), out of your unborn child. Remember, it's not about you but the child.

Make sure that your wife not only eats well, but right. That means you may have to protect her from her family and friends and possibly even herself. Though they may mean well they might try to feed her stuff she doesn't need nor would you want her to eat and or drink. They may give her advice that may not seem sound. Everyone seems to think that a woman during pregnancy must be fattened up. Not true. She just needs to eat right when she's hungry without eating just for the sake of eating. She needs no help gaining and or putting on weight. Her body will naturally do it. It needs no help. Besides, both of you want her to be able to recover and have a decent body after childbirth I am sure so don't put her in a position where later she remarks that she must have thrown her body away. Conversely, don't curtail her eating during pregnancy either as that is worst. She's eating for two or if pregnant with twins three you know.

Please be sure you have chosen a good doctor and medical facility that will be the place your child is born. Try to have a natural childbirth. Don't force the child to be born. When the child is ready it will come out on its own unless something is wrong in which case please listen to your doctor. If something is really wrong, natural goes out the window, as now you must save the child and your spouse both! Preferably choose a doctor that is both into what is natural yet proficient with conventional medicine. It's best to have the best of both worlds. Make sure the good doctor does not have a problem with you being in the room when the child is born. You should and must be there through the whole thing unless it just can't be helped. Remember, that is your baby to and you are both going through this pregnancy together. Although you can't carry a baby, that doesn't make you any less a parent.

During pregnancy, make sure that your woman knows not only that you love her but also appreciate her. Be consistent. As a matter of fact, start this before pregnancy and do it consistently for all of her life. This will assuage her fears and out of whack hormones during pregnancy. No fat jokes no matter how much of a sense of humor she normally has. Massage her often. Bathe her often. Talk to her as often as you can. It will make her feel good and make things go well. Of course do these things within reason and as normal as possible as you don't want to put her on a high and then she wonders what happened later. Henceforth keep this in mind, how you start is how you must finish. Don't just do it for the pregnancy then stop! As I was saying, do these things and make sure she knows how wonderful you really think she is on a regular basis. Carrying a child can really play havoc with a woman's emotions. Some worst than others so you may have to get ready for a long ride. Not to mention, don't be surprised if you feel the pains your woman feels while carrying the child. There is a special spiritual connection between you and your woman and you will be surprised at what you may feel. She's carrying the baby but you are both pregnant.

Now while this is going on you need to child proof your home. If you have a glass table, you are going to want to store it away and replace it with a **sturdy** wood table that is not painted with anything toxic. Babies like to chew on just about everything.

Do you have lots of glassware? Store it away and get non-toxic plastic cups. Get clear or opaque glass look a likes. I don't care how pretty they are just get the glass out of the way. Got stuff around that can be a choke hazard. They have got to go to. If it's breakable, it must not be within reach or climbable reach of a child. Never ever underestimate the ability of a child to reach anything. Mine could have put any rock climber to shame.

Take your time to investigate and get a good baby seat, play pen and crib for your child or children if you have double the trouble on the way. Make sure they are good and sturdy. Don't be cheap. Once your child or children has outgrown them they should be stored away not thrown away. You never know, you may need them again one day. Even if you don't, your kids or another family member may have children of their own one-day and it would be far better for these things to get further use rather than be in a land fill somewhere.

Play soothing music that you and your spouse both like often. Not only will this sooth the unborn baby but you to. Read to your unborn child, both of you, often. At the very least, the child will get use to both of your voices and be comfortable with them and thus you.

Start researching diapers and related materials you will use on your child's rear and then begin to purchase them or better yet set the money aside for them. I would advise that you get diapers that are non-toxic and biodegradable if possible. This will not only be good for your child but the environment to. On the subject of baby powder, if you can help it, use cornstarch and nothing else. The usage of talcum powder is questionable and at worst can cause serious illness in you and your baby. Information on this can be found on the web. Regarding baby wipes, the fewer chemicals and the more natural ingredients used the better. Try to steer clear of scented baby wipes. The scent may smell good to you but may affect your child's sinuses. Find good natural soaps that will not be hard on you and your child's skin. I will have more on this subject later.

Invest in a good strong vacuum cleaner, carpet steam cleaner and floor steamer mop now! Vacuum cleaners should preferably be bag less. The steam cleaner will be a Godsend to you later for every spill and or accident by your baby. Trust me. The steam mop is great at sanitizing the floors whether carpet or tile.

Get a bathroom trashcan with a lid you can activate with your foot and place it where you will be changing your child's diapers.

Institute the rule that shoes will no longer be worn throughout the home and stick to it. Let no one walk through your home with his or her shoes on. If they have athlete's foot, or just plain unclean feet then make them put on shoe bags at the door. Why do this? Can you remember everywhere you walked during the day? The gas on the bottom of your shoe from the gas station, that gum you stepped in because someone was too nasty and lazy to spit it in the garbage can, that dog crap you accidentally stepped in, etc, etc. Do you really want that on the floor that you, your spouse and ultimately your child and or children may lie on and put your heads on? Let's not forget the parasites you may have picked up on the bottom of your shoe while walking across the ground. Just because you can't see them doesn't mean they aren't there.

Institute rules of upkeep and cleanliness now and live by them if you haven't already. It will make it that much simpler to teach your child and or children later. It's hard to teach a child to have good habits you don't practice yourself.

Get some books on child rearing and discipline and read them now but do not hold them as the definitive word on the subject. No two children are the same. I will have more on this subject later. Choose and get a good baby bed, baby car seat, and apparatus for carrying your child with you while in the store or what have you. Do it now. Don't wait until the baby gets here. Now you can take your time and do it right and make good choices before your baby is through cooking in the oven.

Have you made sure that you are in a good neighborhood worthy of raising children? If not, start making plans now to change that. You don't want to raise your child around other children whom can only be bad influences or you will have to fight every day to deprogram your child.

Document your pregnancy. Why do that? Because it is a moment that will never happen again. Even if your spouse has more children, this particular singular moment will never happen again.

Buy a good juicer and food processor and look into organic baby food. Start buying it now and get ready. Once your child is ready for solid food, it will go quick. That juicer and food processor will become your best friends. Also, glass baby bottles are preferable. Plastic baby bottles must be researched before purchasing as many of them contain chemicals that are bad for your babies' health.

Lastly, be sure that your spouse gets plenty of rest, exercise within reason, exposure to enjoyable things, nutritious food, vitamins and minerals of natural i.e. not artificial origin. You should also be doing the same for yourself. Be sure to get a good book on proper food combining. For instance, fruits should not be combined with proteins when eating as the body digests them differently. The same goes for sugary foods and proteins and or fruits. These rules apply to every one of all ages so do research it. By the way, get stainless steel utensils and cookware. Avoid aluminum and non-stick pans. They are toxic in the long term.

Chapter Three
TheBigDay

B efore your spouse goes into labor, plan for it. She will have to get to the hospital somehow. She will not be in any shape to drive once that water breaks. When it happens she will need you and she will need you now. Be sure you are able to be there and don't lose it when it happens. She will have enough problems and the last thing she will need is to be strong for you and her. It has to be the other way around. For some of you that will be easier said than done but you are a man so get over it.

Hospitals do not have friendly parking plans. The parking is great if you are a doctor but for patients and particularly men trying to get their laboring wives, girlfriends, whatever to the hospital to have a baby it has been and to my knowledge continues to be the pits. They will tow you quick. No mercy whatsoever so do yourself a favor and figure out the parking shituation, (no, that was not a misspelling), before that day arrives and what you are going to do when you get there. If you are lucky you will be able to call ahead and they will be waiting for her. Make sure you know where they are taking her though as you will be treated as immaterial in finding where they took her.

Once in the room, keep her calm. It could take time despite the fact her water broke. Be there and take part despite needing to stay out of Johnny/Joannie Bench I mean the doctors way. Some doctors are more thoughtful and make sure you have a role in the birth. Welcome it. You won't get the chance again.

Make it clear to the medical staff your wife will be breast-feeding your child or they will stuff your newborn with formula. You do not want this to happen. Formula changes the natural flora of the child's digestive tract and once a child gets use to formula they won't want anything else. Also, that first breast-feeding has a special bonding effect between mother and child. Don't mess that up.

If you can, make sure that the hospital completely destroys the afterbirth immediately. If you don't, some of it may go to a lab somewhere. Insert evil laugh now, no just kidding, maybe.

After your wife is home with the baby, do not expect her to do much for a while. Having a baby takes a toll on a woman. Some of them actually have to get stitches as a result. Let her heal and recover.

Be prepared to do the cooking. I don't care if she was the one who did all the cooking, Mr. Dad that's going to be your job for awhile now and no the garbage at the fast food joint they call food does not constitute providing nourishment for your budding family so if you really love them as you profess feed them properly. Yes, I said them. Whatever your spouse eats so does your baby by way of the mother's breast milk.

So in closing, keep them fed well, keep the home environment clean and do not allow your wife to become stressed out. Yes, being a good real father is not easy but later you will find it rewarding. No one can do your job. Only you can so do it well.

Side Note:

Once a baby is born all the way up to the age of 1 3 to maybe 1 5, children are in their formative years. The cut off age varies up to 1 6 and 1 7 but in all practicality once a child reaches 1 3 or 1 4 years old it is almost over. You may be able to do a few modifications 1 4 to 1 5 but after that unless the child recognizes a few things themselves they need to change its over. So be sure and teach them good morals, characteristics and responsibility now while you can. As much as possible do not spoil them. Keep disruptive influences at bay. Such influences could even be your own family. Family has a way of undoing all the good you may be trying to accomplish with your children. They mean well but you can mean well and still hurt someone. In a nut shell, it's too late to try to properly raise a child once they get a lot older so don't dote, spoil, and overlook issues because you think its cute or no big deal and then when you discover at 1 2 on up you have a monster you decide you are going to properly parent. It doesn't work.

Chapter Four
That Helpless Baby

Baby is here. Baby is now king or queen and you and your spouse's lives are now theirs unless you plan on being bad parents. I hope you are ready. Babies do not reason. They only know that they need. You must care for and love the baby without spoiling it. There is no one middle point to this that can be figured out. No to children will be the same and you will be searching for that happy medium with a broken flashlight in the dark but you will eventually find it. There is a book that helps you understand what each cry means. You will want to purchase it. I will list it later.

For a while, your baby will only be able to drink milk. Make sure that your spouse drinks plenty of water as well as juices, preferably organic. This is essential to breast milk production. Absolutely no soda water, I don't care if it is organic and has non refined sugar no. No junk. This is important; as it will affect the child's eating habits even though they are not the ones consuming the junk.

Get a breast pump if you haven't already. Your wife's breast may hurt sometimes with the amount of milk that may be in them. Now you will be glad you bought those bottles, as she will be able to aspirate her extra milk into them. Have her fill them only 3/4ths full though. Why? Remember that juicer you bought? It is now time to put it to work if you haven't already done so. With the 1/4th space left over, juice some banana and apple for starters. You may have to take a spoon to get it out of the juicer and into the bottle but that is ok. It will be thicker than just milk so you will need to take a needle to slightly enlarge the hole on the bottle nipple enough so that baby can suck out the contents but yet under normal circumstances it does not spill on its own. The fiber and extra nutrition along with momma's milk will be good for the baby. This will also, get baby use to what will come later. You can put different combinations into that 1/4th but use banana as a base. Hence, always first juice one banana, then you can do things like broccoli, carrots, and green bell pepper. If you juice watermelon it must be by itself without banana. Melons as a rule should be eaten alone no matter what your age. My daughter's baby sitter and my best friend always had the most interesting looks while I was doing this. The bottles that went with my daughter to day care came in a variety of colors. Whitish yellow if it was just straight breast milk with banana, orange due to carrots, green and purple, and also red due to water melon. My daughter enjoyed them all and they were good nutrition. Also, let's say baby starts to develop a slight cough. Don't wait for it to become full blown, with your chosen vegetable mixture, juice 1/3 red onion and a clove of garlic. Shake the bottle well afterward. Baby will hardly notice thanks to the banana and other vegetables. I can't guarantee it, but usually it will knock it out. By the way, you can try various combinations, not just the ones I mentioned. It's all good.

Talk often to your child. I mean talk, not the goo goo gaga baby talking. The more you talk normally to your children, the better their own communication skills will be. Also, unless they are in danger of hurting themselves, never suppress the child's efforts at movement and exploration. This is essential to their development.

Chapter Five
A Cleaner Way for Your Baby to Benefit from Their Diaper Change

Now about cleaning baby when they use the restroom. Most people think changing a diaper is taking off the old used diaper, wiping with a baby wipe, throwing on some powder and a new diaper and presto you're done. Ummm NO! The diaper rash ointment manufacturers are going to love you if that's all you do. There is a better way. Unless your child has medical issues this should work. When you are preparing to change your child, always place two soft thick towels for that purpose next to the sink. One will be for when you start and the other will be for when you finish and are putting a fresh diaper or pull-up on your baby. Be sure to place the fresh diaper or pull up on your finishing towel before you start. Now place the baby on their back facing you on the towel you will always use to start from. Now turn on the water in the sink and make sure it has a comfortable temperature for your baby. Next, unclip the diaper. If they had a BM, use a baby wipe to get rid of as much of the residue as possible and then wash your hands. Now lift your baby straight up and out of the diaper and place the baby into the palm of your right hand on their stomach. With your left hand throw away the old diaper. Still holding the baby with your right hand, ease the baby into the water and rinse well. Now pick up the soap with your left hand and lather that hand up well. Now put the soap down and use your lathered up left hand to thoroughly wash your babies' private area. If you don't want to use your hand to do the bathing then use a washcloth. Just be sure to change that washcloth every day. Now rinse your left hand and rinse your baby thoroughly in the running water from the sink. Now wash your left hand. This is where you really want liquid soap handy as you only have two hands. Once you have done that you can now place the baby in your left hand facing up on their back. Now rinse again. This way you make sure that your baby is totally clean. Now place your baby on the towel you designated for finishing and dry them well. Now wash your hands. After drying your hands properly place baby on the diaper and use a baby wipe to take care of any moisture you may have missed. Now apply baby oil and powder. Seal the diaper. You're done. This may sound like a lot to do but actually it isn't. This is very comfortable for babies as opposed to how most people normally change diapers. So long as I used this little technique let's call it the "McNeil Baby Diaper Change Technique" my children never ever developed diaper rash. One day my grandmother came over and told me I didn't know what I was doing and for two days had me do it the way most people do. Suddenly, before I knew it, my child had developed diaper rash. It goes without saying I went back to my own way and never had that problem again. Remember, use a good natural soap. There are a few choice ones that I use that I purchase from stores that provide these soaps. The great thing about the natural soaps is that you don't feel a film still upon yourself as with the petrol-derived soaps which are really detergents. Also, do not use hand sanitizer on your baby at all whatsoever. They will poison your child. I'd shy away from liquid soaps too unless they are natural and easy to rinse off. If you use such, be sure it's easy to rinse off as there is nothing worse than trying to rinse off soap and realizing its still on your skin. Your baby doesn't have the luxury of saying, "Hey! The soap is still there. It's itching me!" They can only cry and you won't know why until it produces an effect you can see.

Chapter Six
What to Do When Baby gets Teeth and Bites During Breast Feeding

Eventually, your baby is going to get their first teeth. One by one they will start to poke up through their gums. That day will be heralded with a yell or other descriptive adjectives by your spouse during breast-feeding when baby decides to try out their new tooth on her. The moment the baby does this try <u>lightly</u> tapping the baby on the forehead with your index finger and firmly say NO!!! Don't yell nor scream for this will probably terrify the baby and negate the message you are trying to send to the baby. Every time this happens, the mother and or you must do this. It may take a couple of days, but the baby will quickly get the message and stop. Particularly if the breast is removed just before that very light tap occurs. The mother should also look the baby in the eyes and say firmly yet lovingly, "Ouch that hurts"

Notes

Chapter Seven
Solid Food

Once those teeth start coming in, it's time to start considering solid food. Organic baby foods are the best, as usually they contain no refined sugar, however, always read labels before you buy and check expiration dates. The best thing to do regarding baby foods is to use them as a base. This is where your food processor comes in. You can take some of a meal you cooked, like beans, enchilada, etc and put it in the food processor with the baby food say, squash, green beans etc and make a more full meal once the food processor is through with it for baby. You can also add mineral supplements suitable for babies to this and baby will never know they took it. As time goes by, baby will be able to eat less processed food. Be sure that you give your baby plenty of water suitable for their age and size. Also, give your baby water 15 to 30 min before feeding them. It will help them better with digestion. You will know by their stool if you are not giving them enough water. Trust me. They may be hard to clean if there is not enough water in their systems resulting from constipation. Constipated babies have a tendency to be irritable to. Trust me, you don't want your baby to be irritable.

Notes

Chapter Eight
Daycares

At some point you will probably need to worry about putting your child in a daycare. Investigate several before choosing one. Come with significant other if necessary but ask to see the daycare facilities. They should give you a tour without asking for you to come back later. If they will not you should move on. Look to see how clean they are, do the children there seem to be happy? If you are raising your child vegetarian do they have issues with that? Do they have issues with your child receiving the breast milk of its mother rather than cow's milk and formula? If they do, move on. Don't waste another minute. If you are like me and decided to provide all of the food baby will eat rather than what they are feeding the rest of the kids find out if they have a problem with it now. If they do, once again move on. Don't plead the point. If they have hang ups and issues with you because you are not doing what the average parent does there are going to be problems later. Also, find out how well they screen their employee's and see if they do anything to enrich the children while they are there. By the way, make sure the kids have a safe place to play both inside and outside. One thing you should be alert for is that no child is left to be by their self at no time. One way to catch that is know when children are taken out to play and make a sudden visit. This has happened to me. It made me change my work hours so that my child wouldn't have to be in a daycare center but I digress, as everybody cannot do that.

Ok, so you found a good daycare. If you have a job with funny work hours or puts high demands on your time you better not only have a good idea of when the daycare closes but plans in place you can't make it before then. If you can get some kind of understanding with them if that is possible and get to know the staff very well. If the daycare closes and your child is there past closing time and you and or your significant other hasn't picked up that baby the daycare is going to call child protective services. It won't matter to them that you or your significant others boss demanded that you or her stay past the time you were suppose to get off. Once they are in your mix they are in there. So make sure that either your job knows you must pick up your child or make sure someone reliable that you trust will without fail.

This brings up another point. If you know that your significant other is unreliable, you must be no matter what. If not, you may be blind-sided. Take no chances. You don't want to get off work to find the authorities waiting for you wondering why your child wasn't picked up. They will not care about whose responsibility it was to pick up the child. So if you know she's unreliable take no chances. If this happens you had better have gotten an understanding with and gotten to know the staff well in which case they will be more than likely to call you and tell you "Hey, no one has come to pick up your child. Will you be coming to pick them up?" That gives you the chance to say, "Yes, I will be there right away", and then you drop everything and make a bee line to pick up your child. If you ever find yourself in that shituation, (no that is not a typo), I should not have to tell you no matter what, go get your child right then and there and profusely thank the daycare employees for alerting you that your child wasn't picked up by your significant other so that you could come right away and remedy the shituation, (hey, I think that word needs to be put in the dictionary). Yes, it may get you in trouble with your job but that's preferable to the child being taken away by and you answering to the authorities. I hope it never happens to you but if it does never ever trust your significant other or whomever to do the right thing regarding your child or children again. They didn't call the daycare and say they'd be late. They didn't call you and say they'd be late. If something happened, why didn't they call you or a family member for help? If their car broke down why didn't they call for a family member to go get the child? Ok, maybe there was no one to call, why didn't they call you? Ok, maybe you have a job you can't receive incoming calls, why didn't she call the job and say it's a family emergency? Ok, your job is run by flaming out right devils that don't give a shit and won't put her in contact with you, there are cabs. If I can think of all this and you can, (you can can't you?), why couldn't she or whomever the responsible party is and or was? Like I said, you can be married and still be a single parent. Be prepared for every possibility.

Chapter Nine
Walking and Hazards for Babies

Now, before they have the ability to crawl, most babies start trying their legs out. Encourage this. The more they do it, the stronger those legs get. Eventually, they begin to pull themselves up and stand while holding on to things. Eventually, they are able to walk but don't have the courage to do it without holding onto something. Encourage them without pushing too fast. Once they got it, they will be going everywhere. Be sure you watch them closely while they are doing this lest they go somewhere or get into something you would rather them not and get into a lot of trouble in the process. It is important that throughout the process you don't carry them everywhere. Yes, I know you love them but love them by making them do as much as possible on their own. Do not lock them in the swing and or baby pin for instance. These things have their uses but it is unhealthy to have them in them all of the time.

Once they can walk do not, I repeat do not carry them around anymore. Make them walk. You'd be surprised at what those young legs can do. Once they can walk well without your help, you can walk into the store with them right by your side. Not on your side. Do not be one of those parents with children whom can probably outrun them hanging on their sides or residing in strollers and baby carriages. I never used these things as I viewed them as impediments to their development. Before my children could walk I had a special strap on pouch for babies so they could be on my back or face away from me in front. They could see everything and not preclude the use of my hands and arms. The moment they could walk though, they were walking. A child use to being packed everywhere will soon be a nuisance to you because they will be use to that and not understand why they have to walk. I'm not saying; never carry a child, because sometimes it is necessary. Just be sure it is a minimum and there is no choice but to do so.

Once they can walk, teach them about hazards early. Like cars and other vehicles, stoves, fire places, sharp implements, equipment that can hurt them, the hazards of climbing bookshelves and dressers and also electricity and wall sockets for instance. Start young. Don't worry whether or not they understand they will get that these things may be dangerous and thus increase the chances they will leave the things you warn them about alone. Do still watch them as their curiosity may still get the best of them. When it comes to poisons around the home don't just teach them and warn them, get some Mr. Yuk stickers and use them. I believe those are still available so look them up. Get child locks to keep them out of things also. One example would be the special hinges you can put inside your cabinets that make it rather difficult for your children to get into them. Do not store anything dangerous on their level ever. Anything that is poisonous and harmful should be stored in a locked cabinet that cannot reached by a child.

Chapter Ten
Potty Training

O hjoy. You will need to have lots of patience. Truck loads of it. Don't yell. For the record, girls are easier to potty train than boys. But for both, start early, start early, start early. Even before they can walk, try to figure out when they need to use the restroom and put them on the potty. Make sure they know what you mean when you ask them "do you have to use the restroom?" Once they can walk, up the ante. The sooner they can go to the restroom instead of having a diaper the better for you, them and your pocket book. You will have to make your little ones comfortable with sitting on a make shift toilet until they can sit on a real one without falling in.

Do not be the one whom tells them when they need to use the restroom. Make them the ones whom tell you when they need to use the restroom. When you awake them or you awake in the morning or both, take them to the restroom right away. This will train the child to do so.

If your child is bedwetting, don't give them any fluids 3 hour before they go to bed. Ask them do they feel themselves needing to use the restroom at night and if so why don't they get up and go to the restroom? **It** may be that they are afraid which is an issue you will have to deal with using a nightlight. Actually, during potty training use a night-light anyway. Your child may not admit to you that they are scared of the dark leaving you scratching your head on the bedwetting issue. Hence, do whatever you can to intercept this issue.

Note: Before I go into discipline, understand this: A parent's job in relation to their children is not only to teach, take care of and protect them, but also protect them from themselves. That is a concept you should never forget. You are the parent not their best friend.

Chapter Eleven
Early Discipline and Later Discipline: When They Can Walk Around and Cause Havoc

How you start is how you finish. Do not use separate forms of discipline for girls and boys. Always use the same disciplinary actions for both. Always! If you do not, you can create a new negative situation between brothers and sisters. Also, just as every rose has its thorn's your beautiful angel of a daughter can become every bit of a terror as a boy can. Girls are tougher to deal with, once out of control for the shear fact they are girls and how society perceives them. So be careful how you correct their behavior, hence, don't discriminate between the two ever. The consequences of a boy for a particular action should be the same for a girl whom commits that same action and vice versa.

If you start off spoiling your child expect to have a monster later, however, don't be a tyrant either when disciplining. Be firm and consistent. Make sure the child knows the rules and the consequences of failure to follow those rules. No whipping. If the child does something wrong, tell them no. If they do it again then tell them the consequences for their actions such as, I will put you in the corner or I will give a pop on the hand, (a soft pop, nothing painful), or I will take away your favorite toy. They do it a 3rd time carry out your threat and don't apologize no matter how hard they scream and cry. Once the screaming, kicking and crying begins tell them if they don't stop right then you will take something else away. They must understand that no means no.

Later Discipline when they can walk around and cause havoc

What do I mean by havoc? Try walking into the living room only to discover your little mighty mite has taken the baby powder and sprinkled it all over your couch and your couch is not leather or you discover your DVD drive stuffed with oatmeal or grits. Mind you, you have already told your child playing with these things is off limits and the child knows this and you know it as the child gives you that "Oh Sh-look" the moment they notice you just caught them in the act. What do you do? The absolutely no spankings crowd is going to tell you put them in time out. Don't spank that child. Hummm. Time out is not just time out for a child. It's also time out for you too. Some children after say age 3-4 are not going to sit in that corner unless you take time out with them and keep them there. However, don't haul off because if you do you just might lose it. So what do you do?

First, get your composure and take away all materials they are using to mess up. Make them sit down away from you and anything else they can get into trouble with you about on the other side of the room. By them not being able to get into trouble and being away from you while within your sight you can cool off and they can calm down. Make it clear to them in a firm way without going overboard that you are really angry, (don't you wish you could say you're truly pissed), with them and you have to cool off while you decide what their punishment will be. They can see you on the other side of the room and now they have time to think, "Oh man, dad's really mad at me. I wonder what's he going to do to me", while you on the other hand can watch them and make sure they don't do anything else and can cool off so that you don't lose it and maybe hurt the child. Maybe not physically but mentally with what you might say that you will later wish you hadn't. You don't want to do that as it has lasting results on the child's psych. Instead, once you cool off, as best you can depending on the age of the child, make them clean it up. If they can walk, grab stuff and make a mess they can clean it up. After that and you have finished any cleaning they may not be able to do, now give them a few pats on the hand that are non-painful and tell them not to do it again. The child will be hurt all the same because they know they did wrong. What you are aiming for is for the child to think, "Gee, I had to work and clean it up and then I got punished for it. I'm not doing that again it wasn't worth it" verses "Gee, I had fun making that mess and all I had to do was sit in a corner for a little while. Hmmm. I'm going to do that again".

Temper tantrum problems. Nip it in the bud now. Example: Your son or daughter can't get their way so they throw their heads or themselves at the floor. Of course you catch them every time so they don't hurt themselves. They usually give you just enough time to catch them. This is what you do. Warn them you are not going to do that again and keep your word. This worked with my son. Just when I thought all had failed, when he again through his head at the floor, he conveniently hit his head. As a result of me not catching him, he looked at me like he wanted to curse me out as though to say, "How dare you!@#$%!! let me hit my head on the floor/ground?" He had only to do that one more time before that never happened again. He learned a hard lesson shall we say. You must make sure the child knows you are the boss not them. If they grow up thinking they are the boss you've got major problems coming and that's an understatement. You have single mothers right now whom are afraid with good reason of their teenagers because of this. Don't ever lose control of your child nor ever let them remotely think they are in control and running the show.

Make sure at all times they know what the rules are and what is expected of them so that there is no confusion and stick to it. At no time should they have the ability to boss you around, nor talk to you like you are a child. Never ever tolerate such behavior. They must grow up respecting you at all times or there will be serious issues with you and your child later.

Notes

Chapter Twelve
To Spank or Not To Spank

Remember in the bible "Spare the rod, spoil the child"? I don't think they meant abuse the child. Right now, there is a big whoop de do about whether or not it is ok to spank your child. Proponents of the never ever spank a child group refer to spanking as hitting your child making it sound like you are using them for a punching bag. Proponents in the spanking camp say, "Hey, I was spanked and I turned out alright!" and they don't agree at all with the do not spank crowd, however, no child should be spanked for every little thing they do. My personal feeling is that the right course lies along a gray line in the middle of both camps leaning more towards the do not spank camp. A child that is constantly spanked for everything will either be a resentful rebellious child or a broken one without confidence. It is far better to find creative ideas of how to achieve the same results of spanking without hitting or using physical force if you can. That also includes not committing psychological abuse which can cause long term psychological damage that can be worst than physical abuse. The damage that is done to a young mind may never heal and last a life time causing negative consequences for the child all of their life.

For the record let's be fair to the spanking crowd. Most in that crowd that I know do not believe in spanking a child for every little thing though there are people like that out there unfortunately. As a matter of fact, new recent research shows that children whom do get spanked are more likely to be successful in school and go on to complete college. However, if the child is spanked as a teenager, they are less likely to do well and may develop social problems. Based on the study, if the child hasn't been spanked before 6 years old do not do it as it will be psychologically damaging to the child and no child in their late teenage years say 16 or so should be getting physically disciplined unless absolutely necessary. If you are going to use spanking as part of your methods of discipline it should start around the age of one and continue with decreasing frequency as the child ages and gains maturity into their teenage years.

I've listened to the "don't spank ever crowds" theories on the radio and TV and have come to some observations and theories of my own based on experience. I've met parents in that crowd and their children have been little terrors. Not all of them but a great deal of them have been. Observationally, back in the day when I was a kid before all of this "do not spank ever commotion" became vogue, children were more in control in the class room and without. It was unheard of to hear of a student jumping on a teacher, their parents, and or challenging authority as they do now. As a matter of fact, your parents were quite familiar with the neighbors and vice versa and if you did something especially bad, your neighbors would tell on you and when your folks got wind of it, it was on. In some cases the neighbors were such good friends with your folks as back in my father's day, you got a spanking from them and then your folks once they found out. So back then you really didn't want to mess up and get your rear double tanned. As a matter in fact, your parents would tell you to go out and get the very switch that was to be used on your behind and you'd better bring back a good one because if you didn't they'd go out and get the whole branch and tear you up with it. Needless to say you thought twice about doing whatever you did that got you that whipping in the first place.

Nowadays, kids are hip to the new laws and regulations. Your child can now do something really bad and threaten you that if you try to do something about it, in fact anything about it, they will just call the child protective services, (yes, some children know exactly who and what number to call, they've got it memorized), say you abused them somehow or not even that. All they have to do is just say you spanked them for doing something wrong and that can be enough to get you hauled off to jail or at least have you under serious scrutiny. I think this sends a really bad message to children. The message that they can run amok and there will be no consequences. Think I'm going too far with that conclusion? Have you looked at the news reports lately? Some of these children will even jump on and fight their own parents and if the parent defends themselves the authorities more than likely will haul them, the parents that is, off to jail. Not the youth that jumped on them in the first place. What's wrong with this picture? Its one thing if parents are abusive and brutalize their children but it is another if the children are the abusers. Just what are parents to do in this situation if they can't stop their children from these actions because to do so will land them in jail or have CPS knocking on their door?

Don't get me wrong, if you are abusing your children you very much should be hauled off. However, the definition of child abuse needs an overhaul lest we be ruled by and live in fear of our own children whom know or will know it's ok for them to get away with and do anything they like because you can't do anything about it.

Worst, you can't disciple your child, but when they get older the police can beat the crap out of them and then try to hold you responsible for the child's actions. The child may really do something bad at school and have to go to court and or juvenile. Oh, by the way, you have to accompany said child to court. The judge will wonder why you allowed the child to be out of control. I know as I've personally witnessed other parents go through it. Now you know back in the day if you screwed up like that your folks would have been ready to kill you, hence you were to afraid to even consider doing anything that stupid unless of course you were a fool anyway in which case you wouldn't be reading this book today.

I guess by now you've figured out I'm not a card carrying non-spanker, however, I don't firmly ascribe to spanking at the drop of a hat either. I think spanking should be a last resort. I repeat, spanking should be a very last resort until children get a lot older, teens for instance in which case there should no longer be a need for such punishment unless you have absolutely no choice. It should be a very rare thing such that the child is more concerned about disappointing you. Why, because there must be an ultimate punishment. A nuclear option shall we call it. There must be. Children are not stupid and unless you have one of those rare children whom only want to try to do good, they constantly push the limits of the envelope to figure out what they can get away with. They study you constantly to figure out what your buttons are and how many they can push before setting you off. They want to know what makes you tick and how to outsmart you. Hence, you must always stay 2 and 3 steps ahead of them. In the beginning this is not hard and can be amusing, but as they get older if you don't watch out they may surprise you.

By the way, children whom get too many spankings get use them and spanking becomes useless. They will just take the spanking and go on doing whatever got them in trouble in the first place. Like I said, they should be rare if used at all and spankings that physically harm the child are child abuse. What you are aiming for is a child whom is more afraid of doing wrong and disappointing you rather than being afraid of receiving punishment. You want them to do right because they want to and it's the right thing to do, not because they will get punished if they do wrong.

What I have figured out is that you first must make sure they know the rules so there is no excuse for not knowing what is wrong and right. Post them if you have to then explain to them your expectations. Besides, children generally know if they 'are doing something wrong. As a matter of fact, they generally know they are about to do something wrong before they set out to do it. Remember back in the day when you were a child? Didn't you usually know something you got in trouble for was wrong before you did it? Remember, the Creator stated in the holy book that the knowledge of right and wrong is written into the hearts of all mankind. Need proof of that. If you see someone starving on the side of the road and you have food with you, what would you do? Mind you, I'm assuming you are not an evil selfish person when I ask that.

If your child acts up or does something they have no business doing tell them no and remind them of the rules you have set forth for them. If the child does it again despite your efforts, tell them no and warn them of the consequences such as the removal of privileges, confiscation of favorite toys or games or a slight pop. If the threat fails then it is time to go through with the threat and do not apologize for it. It is punishment. Never ever threaten to punish a child for something they do wrong repeatedly despite your efforts of asking them not to do it and then fail to carry out the punishment. Never. You must always be consistent. Inconsistency will send the wrong message and the child will begin to not take you seriously. If you never carry out your threats of discipline, the child will not only fail to take you seriously but will also one day consider you not worthy of their respect, and consider themselves your equal and at worst your master.

Every child needs to know if they do something wrong there are consequences for what they did and shall be all of their lives. If you steal you go to jail. If you speed you will receive a ticket. If you physically hurt someone you may go to prison. Kill someone you will go to prison, for life or be placed on death row. If you are late to your job too many times you are fired. If you don't do your job you are fired. If you have no job you can't pay your bills nor buy the things you want. Without income you can't pay your bills, eat and will lose your home. So the same must be taught to your children within the boundaries that they live in, in order to be prepared for what will come when they reach the outside world.

Trust me, if they grow up out of control there will be someone to put some control on them later and those people will not love them nor care about them. Tazer, billy club and or street justice anyone?

As for the time out crowd, what I have found out about time out is it does not work with all children. Some will stay in time out but others will not. This forces you to make them stay there to enforce it. In such cases you are both in time out. Kind of defeats the purpose. It worked with my children the first few times until they figured out they could leave if no one stuck around to make them stay in time out. My daughter would try to sneak out of it and my son would just physically force his way out of time out any way he could. Time out just didn't work for my children period; however, when I tried to institute it was when they were older like 5 and 9. The cases I have seen it work for others were when the children were much younger. It depends on the child and when the use of time out was instituted. If instituted early the chances are good it will work, but if your children are not use to it and are older it will more than likely not work. Some children would have to be chained to something to keep them in time out without your enforcement in which case that undeniably would be child abuse. I repeat, if the child is raised from birth before they can even walk on time out I can see how it may work, but if you are instituting it at a later age I believe you are going to have problems. If you combine time out with removing something extremely important to the child should they try to escape from it, then maybe I can see it working, but if there is no such thing then I think it probably will not. In other words there must be a consequence for them trying to circumvent time out.

The threat of the belt and or switch has worked though for quite some time. As a matter of fact, switches are more effective than belts. Just the mere presence of a switch or the threat you will get one inspires a positive reaction from children. Children whom have never heard the word switch uttered nor seen one somehow know what a switch is. The denial of being able to use the computer and removal of the X Box, Play Station or what have you are very effective methods also. Not being able to see their friends nor being able to talk to them on the phone has worked on my children, not to mention taking of the cell phones too. Total denial of phone and computer privileges really gets to older children such as teens. Not being able to go outside, go to the park, the movies or to visit friends has done wonders with all children. Increases in chores temporarily as punishment has an effect as well. The treat that you will permanently take away something that they love and mean it does wonders too!

Notice how many times in that last paragraph I mentioned spanking compared to everything else. I didn't eliminate it but I didn't take if off the table either. No two children are the same. One will be nice and quiet but sneaky; the other will be loud and like a challenge overtly. Another will be all around nice and only occasionally get themselves in minor trouble. Another will be hell bent on having their way be damned whoever gets in their way. There is no one way to parent and discipline. There is no one size fits all method to keeping your children in check. You have got to be ready for whatever personality the Creator and ultimately you and' your significant other bestowed upon your child and or children. You will not get a second chance to get it right with any one particular child, so you've got to get it right the first time as best you can. Remember the Creator has a sense of humor, (remember yourself as a child, guess what, the parents curse works doesn't it), and use the best tools and techniques at your disposal with much love and patience.

Note: Never discipline a child when you are livid. Tell the child to go to another room or something while you mull over what they did and decide what to do with them. This does several things.

1. The wait will get to the child. Like I said before, if you have made sure beyond doubt they know right from wrong, the child will be fully aware they screwed up. The knowledge that they screwed up is going to play through their minds with wonderment of what you will do to them. That wait by itself will be a form of punishment. The anticipation of the consequences of their actions.

2. You get to cool off and reasonably consider what to do. When you are livid you consider things in a very passionate manner. You never want to passionately meet out punishment, whatever it may be, if you can help it. At that point, your nerves are raw and it won't take much else to set you off in a bad way. Particularly if you have one of those children whom want to challenge everything. One of those could send you off the deep end.

3. Once you have cooled off you can formulate a manner of discipline that more perfectly fits the child's offense. Maybe it wasn't as bad as it seemed at first once you've cooled off. For instance, what if what the child did was purely an accident. It may have been a bad accident but it is still an innocent accident that wasn't intended. In that instance the child will already be feeling pretty bad about what happened. Those things happen. The child needs to be talked to about it and or taught so that it never happens again but certainly not punished. They will already be punishing themselves inside. The exception of course would be if it was something even a blind man could see would be wrong. Every child has some good sense, (some more than others), and they should be taught to use it.

Notes

Chapter Thirteen
Food and Nutrition

Start your children on the path of eating properly from day one. How you start is usually how you finish. Do not give children sweets of any sort until they are at least 4 years old.

Actually, the older they are before introduction to junk food the better. The earlier they are introduced to sweets the more likely they will be junk food junkies. Also, never give your child soda water particularly when they are at a young age. The acids in the soft drink will eat at their young tooth enamel. Also, you want them to drink water. If you introduce them to soft drinks, particularly at a young age, they will not want to drink water due to the fact that water does not have a taste.

So, only give your children water and 100% real juices. They will be introduced to the bad stuff soon enough once they start school and your family gets a chance to spoil them. Also, an alternative to soda water are carbonated organic fruit juices, (these are really good and they only have the sugar Mother Nature intended), and soft drinks in markets that have them that are only composed of natural ingredients and raw unrefined sugar.

Do not give your children white bread. It is much better for them to eat whole grain bread. As a matter of fact white flour and refined sugar products should be avoided at all cost. Refined sugar has been shown to decrease the memory and effectiveness of the immune system of those whom ingest it.

Be sure that you feed your children a variety of foods that are good for them. Do not feed them a mono diet of food as the nutrients they need are contained in the variety of foods that the Creator provided for us upon this Earth. Also, don't just cook for one day. Cook enough food that will last for several days and if necessary you can put in the freezer and utilize later. An example would be a large pot of rice, beans, vegetables, etc. Brown rice in particular as it takes awhile to cook, yet is so much better than white rice. Given work hours and children going to school these things must be taken into consideration.

Lastly, never let your children dictate to you what they will and will not eat. You are the parent, not them. A child will refuse to eat something they have never had based on looks or what they heard someone else say. Remember, you have to protect your children from all dangers including themselves. If a child could have their way and you did not teach them right, they would eat only macaroni and cheese, cookies, candy, pastries, hot dogs, cheese pizza, burgers and fries every day until their bodies shut down and they collapsed with a sweet cake in their mouths.

Chapter Fourteen
Morals and Manners

Start teaching children morals early. The teaching can be direct or indirect but do it. The moment they can hold a bar of soap, teach them to wash their hands as soon as they come from outside, use the restroom, get through playing and before they eat whether they are at home, some else's home or at a restaurant. Teach them to brush their teeth after each and every meal unless they are in a situation where that is not possible. Teach them to take a bath/shower every night before going to bed. Teach them to clean up period particularly behind themselves if they make a mess. Teach them as early as possible to treat others as they wish to be treated. Teach not to be selfish and that it is ok to share within reason. Teach them it is bad to steal and ask them how they would feel if someone took something from them. Teach them not to hit others lest they be hit themselves. Teach them to be honest, but in the course of doing so don't ever lie to them or you will have negated what you are trying to teach them. Teach them empathy for others within reason. I say within reason as you don't want your child to be a floor mat for others to walk on, so teach them discernment as well once they can understand the concept.

How to teach discernment? You will have to use real life situations. Trust me others will give you plenty of opportunities to do this. You just have to wait for it. For instance you may be trying to get through your child's thick skull why they should not just dart out into the road or through a parking lot. The moment you see a child get hurt on the news, (no I'm not saying it's good to benefit from others misery), by doing the very act you are trying to teach and warn them against say, "See, that is what I was talking about. Would you like that to be you?" If they have a close call use it to your advantage. Instead of punishing them say,

"Remember when I warned you about that? Now it's happened because you didn't listen and did not pay heed to me." The best lessons are the ones we learn just by listening to others whom know better. Unfortunately, despite your best efforts some lessons can only be learned the hard way by your little one. To keep them from getting hurt you may have to actually engineer some incidents without them knowing it to protect them from getting hurt in real ones. No, I am not telling you to do something as crass as almost running over them. Don't be an idiot. I mean engineer something that you have total control over and there is no chance of them getting nothing more than maybe a pinprick. You just want to get their attention as some children are more hard headed than others and must learn the hard way. An example of what I mean is maybe you've been telling them to pick up their toys lest someone step or slip on said toys and hurt themselves. If they don't do what you say remove everything from the area they could seriously hurt themselves on. Make sure the floor is soft and keep everyone else from the offending area and wait. It usually doesn't take long. They will step on their own toy and it will hurt or they will slip and fall. I should not have to tell you to make sure the toy wasn't sharp nor could cut or puncture the skin. You wouldn't by a toy like that would you? Anyway, their pride will be more hurt than any physical hurt they may suffer. Now you have your perfect opportunity to say, "I told you so" instead of yelling at them. Be sure you are smiling when you say it. Your child will learn to hate that phrase. Make "I told you so" a dreaded saying. Every time your child is being hard headed and not doing or taking care of something you told them to do or take heed of tell them, "Ok, don't get mad when I say my favorite saying". Trust me, they will finish that saying for you before you get to. They will usually remedy the problem if for no other reason than to not have to worry about hearing you say, "I told you so", unless they have an especially bad case of rock headedness but I digress. As I was saying though, sometimes you have to let them mess up. After all, it is by mistakes that we all learn. Just make sure that you are there to cushion the fall and or prevent them from really hurting themselves and when its over get in your "I told you so. If you had listened to me this would never have happened. Did you listen to me? Nooo. You just had to learn it the hard way. You won't be satisfied until you kill yourself." And whatever else you can think of that your child will dread hearing you say. Your child will be begging for you to just go on ahead and give them a whooping instead of listening to you drone on. To them, listening to you is going to be worst than actually getting a whipping.

They are going to want you to just shut up. Don't do it. There is nothing worst to a child than screwing up and then you sweetly and kindly making them have to think about how stupid they were without telling them so. Getting the whipping is an easy out for them. If you do it, they get it over with, shut you up because they can say, "come on, you whipped me already", and then they will be back to doing whatever it is they shouldn't have because they didn't learn anything.

So if they do stupid stuff, make them dread your voice and what you will say instead of the switch. However, if they are doing something like being determined to be road kill or something along those lines you might be forced to use the switch because there is no recovery from something like that. If words are not enough to prevent them from getting into severe trouble, enforce belt discipline because if an incident happens there usually is no second chance. Once they are paralyzed, brain damaged or dead that's it. If they are disappearing on you when you are in the store it only takes a second for them to be gone forever.

Let's get back to the subject at hand. Teach them to not be lazy but instead, industrious, prompt and never late. Trust me; you don't want them to develop the habit of lagging all the time and having a "whatever" attitude. Speaking of attitudes, do not allow your children male or female to develop negative attitudes nor be allowed to have such with you. They should know to have respect for you and others whom are in positions of authority. People think this is cute when they are very little and young but later will find it very unpleasant and ugly. They can and often will be labeled for it in school by their teachers. Later in life they could use it on the wrong person and get hurt too. Besides, do you really want to raise a child that has no respect for you and will treat you any kind of way including trying to run you and possibly wanting to jump on you one day when they feel they are big enough and have decided they don't want to hear your stuff anymore and feel they don't need you telling them what to do. However, they are living in your home, eating your food, using your lights and water, wearing the clothes and shoes you bought for them, etc. etc. The moment a child disrespects you and or wants to talk crazy to you address it immediately! Never ever let a child think it is ok to do that. You will regret it the day you do.

Teach family values and roles of girls and boys, men and women early. Given how out of control society is you don't want them to be confused as to what they are suppose to be and what is expected of them. When they are ready you will have to touch on some rather unpleasant topics and realities with them. Just be honest and tell it like it is. Don't sugar coat anything when you do this. The more opportunities for confusion and or undesirable paths they may take in their lives you eliminate the better.

Religion? Church? Masque? Temple? There are too many beliefs and divisions in religion for me to want to touch that. Just be sure to carefully screen all such and make sure they are teaching what you know to be right. There are devils in the pulpits too.

Teach them to love themselves. Make sure that they understand what loving themselves means and what it doesn't. It means loving themselves enough to be clean and want to live in a clean home environment. Teach that in accordance with teaching them to clean up. Teach them they should love themselves enough to have good hygiene and keep themselves clean. Teach them they should love themselves enough to not allow others to take advantage of them and use them. Teach them they should love themselves enough that their clothes look nice and not dirty and rumpled up. Teach them they should love themselves enough that they don't leave the home nasty, hair unkempt, bad breath because they didn't brush their teeth and faces a blind man can see didn't get washed. Teach them that loving you and others is more than saying they love you but also their actions. They must know that actions speak louder than words and if you love and care for someone, their actions must show it. Just be sure they understand you are talking about love in terms of family and friends. They are not ready for anything past that and you don't want them to get the wrong idea. There is plenty of that to go around from the media like what we see on TV every day.

Chapter Fifteen
Television and Video Games

No television until they are 3 and then really limit it and maintain control of what they watch. Seriously, this is super important. Too much TV is very bad. It affects how their minds develop and the kinds of idea's that form in their heads. It also can have really bad effects on their creativity. Children who watch TV tend to be less creative as everything is done right on TV for them and they expect life to be that way. Instant gratification is what it is called I do believe. So carefully regulate the TV time once they are old enough to have it at all. If you don't do this, they will eventually watch things they really shouldn't and you will have a whole new set of problems. Image problems, moral problems, respect problems. For instance, not many people are going to agree with me but would you like your 2-year-old daughter trying to look like and dance like that female pop star doing that single ladies song. Ok, think that's cute. Wait until she decides to do that out in public at the wrong time. Not good enough. Wait until she's 8 or 9 and thinks it's ok to dress up like a hoochie momma and thinks you are wrong because you won't buy her more revealing clothing like her friends whose parents don't care or think it's cute. Cute, that is until their child turns up pregnant in their teens. Am I being dramatic? Look at the statistics and you think about it. No, it's not the only factor in leading up to these things but as a parent every little bit you can do to prevent your budding child from going down these paths counts and adds up. Girls and boys often try out what they see. Don't let the drama on TV get played out in your home. Remember, not only do you have to protect them, but you have to protect them from themselves too.

No, I didn't forget the little boys. You must monitor what they watch also and don't forget the video games. Yes, there is violence everywhere but don't let them play mindless killing games nor watch tons of sex and violence. Whether boy or girl they will become desensitized to these things. You can't keep them from everything however you must use discretion and draw the line somewhere. Little boys tend to like to act out various things. It's normal for them to do so. Just beware of what they are exposed to lest they act out something you definitely would not want them to think is normal and ok to act out. You must give them constant lessons on reality lest they substitute it with the reality that is on TV or in a game.

When it comes to video games, start your children off with video games aimed at educating them yet are fun to play. Beware of video games that are such that the only thing your child can think of is that game. You will know these by a change in your child's behavior and their grades. Some of these are online games hence you must monitor what your child is doing online. As of a matter of fact, carefully monitor what they are doing online period, not just games. Predators have moved their game online and you don't want your child to be one of their victims. Predators are not just pedophiles either. There are online crooks that want to trick you and your child into giving them your personal information so they can masquerade as you or your child. Chances are you know this game but your child probably will not. If they get your child's identity you may be shocked to find out that they have bought a whole bunch of expensive stuff without the child's knowledge and the expense is now yours. What's worse, the child never knew that they bought the stuff. The authorities may be looking for your child for some crime they never committed because such vermin has used their identity. This is a very cold set of humans whom care nothing of whose lives they ruin, even a child's.

Regarding television, the best thing to do once you start allowing TV time is to watch everything they watch. If you are going to have cable, you have to make use of the parental controls. You have to do this in order to know what they are watching. This will give you an idea of what is bad and what is ok. You will quickly find that some things labeled children's programming are ok and some aren't. In fact, some of the cartoons that come on during the day I found to be rather sick and I made sure my children were not watching them. If you forbid something to be watched, be sure and explain why in terms your child understands. If not, whatever you just forbade becomes forbidden fruit. We all know how that story goes.

Make sure they look at something other than cartoons and other kids programming. You really, really, really want them to be interested in watching something other than Disney Channel and Cartoon network. Show them National Geographic, History Channel, Science Channel, Travel Channel, Discover Channel, Discovery Kids, Channel 8, something they will enjoy and learn something. Otherwise they are just watching brain dead TV. I'm not saying don't ever let them watch the kid's only stations but if that's all they watch you are going to have problems. My son for instance loves to watch "The Universe" series with me, which comes on the History Channel. The other stations I mentioned have some really good shows on them as well. Drop the sports channel or whatever it is you are watching to experience these stations with them and you may be surprised at how much you enjoy and learn from them as well. Once again, this is quality time that will never come back again. Every day, hour and minute is precious. You can never purchase another once you have lived it.

The only thing better is turning off the TV and doing a project with your child, (does not matter male or female), that can be something like putting a model plane or rocket together and then flying it or a model boat and sailing it or putting together a doll house or shopping for a fashion set with your daughter. There are all kinds of science kits out there you and your children can get into. Take them to the beach, park, museum, amusement park, etc. Yes, I know sometimes you may want some time to yourself and be left alone but you have to give them some of that time too. Better you than the TV and or video games all of the time. Also, if it is convenient, join them in some outdoor activities or just let them go outside to play. With the obesity rate on the rise, this isn't a bad idea.

Notes

Chapter Sixteen
When Should Your Child go to Bed

Nine pm should be the latest during the school week. In fact 8:30 would be better but make 9pm the limit. Children should get 8 hours of sleep minimum. Doctors have recently said 9 hours optimally for all children. A child's brain develops while they sleep and their bodies grow during this time to. If they don't get enough sleep it affects their ability to think, their moods and also their immune systems. So make sure they get enough uninterrupted sleep. The body actually starts to break down the more it is deprived of quality deep sleep.

To that end, make sure when they go to bed there are no disturbances around them. That means no radios nor television sets should be on in the room they are sleeping in as this disturbs deep sleep and instead puts the body into light sleep which though it looks the same it very much is not. The room lights should not be on either. You must enforce this as children have a tendency to try to monitor you and then sneak and have these things on and or engage in activities like playing games or watching TV. Some children will protest that the radio, TV and or having the lights on helps them go to sleep. Do not allow them to dictate such excuses to you. If you do, you are only allowing them to develop bad habits that you will pay for in problems with the child later that will give you much stress in overcoming. The older they get with this issue the worst it is. You may actually find it a serious struggle later, particularly when it comes to getting them up in the morning to be on time for school, particularly if they must catch the bus or you are dependent upon them to be ready so that not only will you be able to drop them off to school but in the process make it to work on time.

Lack of proper amounts of deep sleep will also affect your child's grades and disposition. Many children whom have behavioral issues once they have had the amount of proper deep sleep corrected improve upon or are no longer prone to bad behavior. It can be like having a different child. Their grades go up as well and they are more attentive.

Besides, once they go to bed you get a well earned break and some you time. Don't take too much though as even though you are an adult, your body needs deep sleep as well.

Chapter Seventeen
When Should You Teach Children Responsibility

Y ou should teach your child responsibility as early as possible and the earlier the better. If you try later when they are older it is going to be a problem. Teach them to clean and be clean early. Teach them how to make their own lunch early. Teach them how to make breakfast early. My son knew how to make grits at the age of 8. Never underestimate what a child can do. Just don't make them slaves and don't give them tasks they may hurt themselves doing. A child is still a child and deserves to be able to enjoy being a child. They must have some kind of chores though.

Even if you are wealthy enough that you can hire a maid, your children should be assigned and taught chores and other responsibilities they will be held accountable for. They should also be taught how to care for and clean up after themselves and the home and be expected to do so. It not only affects their character but their attitude to things and the people in their lives. People like you for instance and yours and their home.

Part of teaching your children responsibility is also teaching them how to be responsible with money. They should have an allowance, however, it should be an earned allowance. Never give children money for doing things they should already do on their own. For instance, do not give children money for chores such as cleaning their rooms, vacuuming and mopping floors and the general upkeep of yours and their yard. These are things they naturally have to do. They live in your home after all. You buy and cook their food, so they should have no problems washing dishes. You wash their clothes, so there should be no issues with them ironing and properly putting up the clothes.

Instead, pay them if they do their grandparents yard for instance. They do not live there and that is work they otherwise would not normally do. Another example is if you are repairing something in the home and they assist outside of their normal duties.

When paying children to do things for what they need and have to do anyway will teach them to have a false since of entitlement. When it comes time to do these very things and no one is giving them anything for it they will be lazy as they are expecting another handout.

Instead, pay them for washing your car, making your bed, cleaning your room, etc.

Don't forget to teach them the value of money. They need to understand how to save money and not buy everything they want. An example of this would be when you take them shopping for clothes, if they want a pair of pants that are more expensive than what you are willing to pay, tell them how much you are willing to pay and tell them they must pay the rest. Teach them to never go into DEBT. As a matter of fact, teach them that DEBT means:

D=   DON'T
E=   EVER
B=   BUY
T=   THINGS

Chapter Eighteen
When Should They Learn to Read and Write

They should learn to read and write as soon as they can handle it. The younger they are able to do so the better. Just don't do it in such a way the child learns to hate it. There are a multitude of books written on the subject. Find out the best ones and read them.

Once you have done so, using your own personal knowledge of your child, develop a plan as to how you will teach your child to read and write and enjoy doing so. Avoid books that have nothing but lots of pictures. Pictures are great, don't misunderstand me, but if that is all your child see's when they see a book, then they are going to want every book to be that way and me and you both know that is not the way it is.

Think of the brain as a muscle. A muscle that does not move but still one that does lots of work. As with any muscle it must be exercised and taught how to do various tasks. In this case various levels of thought processes of which reading and writing are a part of. The young mind must be taught to not only do these things but also comprehend them and the purpose of such.

The way I have explained it to my children is when they read, picture what is being conveyed as though it is a movie playing inside their brains. When you go to the movies you don't just sit there and not know what you are seeing. You take in all the visual and audio information and comprehend it. Through comprehension of all the information being processed by your mind comes enjoyment of the movie. So it is with reading and so it must be taught to your children. One way or another reading is being done and every movie, cartoon, documentary, etc. started as an idea in someone's mind that was then wrote down and translated into its final form.

The earlier you can achieve this with your children the fewer problems you will have with teaching them the necessity of reading and writing. You may have to institute days where there is no TV and or games, at least for a couple of hours, only reading. Be sure to be a good example of a good reader and writer to your children. They will find it worthy of their attention once they see you are living up to what you are preaching to them concerning reading and writing.

Chapter Nineteen
Toys

This is a very important and underrated subject. First of all, before you buy any toy find out where it was manufactured and whether or not it is toxic. The toy may contain lead, antimony and a host of other nasty chemicals as has been reported on the news. You must also make sure it is not a choking hazard.

Now that you've done that, try to get toys that make your child think and use their brains yet are still fun. Lego's for instance was my favorite as a child. Now a day's though, some Lego's come in kits that remove the need for imagination so you have to really look. The point is that if all of your child's toys don't require any imagination and thought from them, then the child's mind becomes lazy and their ability to use their imaginations and be creative and use analytical thought suffers. They will never want to put something together no matter how simple. They will want you to do it. They will tell you they can't think of anything to create and will always want and ask you for your ideas. You will find out how bad this is the first time they need to do a science project for school and you wonder whose project it is, yours or theirs.

I'm not saying everything has to be a brain toy but there better be a healthy dose of them in the mix somewhere for both girls and boys. Make sure all toys are on their level of course. When they get a toy they have to put together they have to read the directions in order to use it. This puts them in the position where they have no choice except to use their reading skills and you should not help them as the idea is for them to use their own mind and creativity. Supervise if maybe there is a chance they could hurt themselves, but that's it. Period. So now they have to read and make theory a practical reality. They have to do problem solving in other words. Once they finish that and have a working toy guess what happens? They will appreciate it more and not only that, they will have improved their ability to think and solve problems. They've exercised that gray matter between their ears. You really want this, really you do. They will need it in school and appreciate you for it latter.

There are plenty of science, electronic, robotic and model kits out there that are fun. Buy kites that have to be assembled. Get artistic kits that require their ideas and imagination. When I was a kid my father got a model car kit I had to make into an actual car. It had an actual motor in it that ran on fuel and came with a remote. Kids today would probably consider me weird but I enjoyed putting it together myself and afterwards I got to enjoy the fruits of my labor by actually driving it. I appreciated it all the more since I alone assembled it and put it together and then watched it work. Don't deny your children the same triumph whether they be girls or boys. Get them as young as you can. There are also erector kits that come with electric motors. Some of them come with you only being able to construct the one figure, which is pictured on the box. Instead try to get the ones where they can construct any number of things they can think of with their own minds and imagination. That's what I had and I do believe such is still available. By the way, puzzles and board games like monopoly and chess are great to.

In a nutshell your mission is to get toys and plaything's that will not stunt the development of your child's mind in any way or fashion yet are still fun and enjoyable! Rather, you must make sure that the mix of playthings you buy for them fulfills the above mission. Find the happy medium that allows you to accomplish that mission.

Also, avoid toys that project an image. Children should develop their own image of self. Not the one projected by a manufacturer. I should not have to elaborate on this one unless you think it is healthy for your daughter to look like and dress like one of those popular dolls that doesn't represent them and your son to think he is any number of violent characters he could never ever be. Don't misunderstand me. We all wanted to be super heroes when we were kids and such but some of the images put out now are disturbing plus in our day we were not bombarded by these images as we are today. I want my child to be themselves and no one else. You should want the same for your child too.

Chapter Twenty
Chores

As soon as the child is mature enough and big enough, they should be gradually given chores. Start off with sweeping the floor and vacuuming. Teach them how to mop. Have them wash the dishes. Teach them how to cut up the vegetables you use to cook. That's their introductory lesson to cooking. Eventually teach them how to properly clean up the restroom and the kitchen. First and foremost teach them to keep their rooms clean. When you know they are ready teach them first how to iron and then how to wash clothes. No, that's not backwards. If you teach them how to wash and dry the clothes first they won't be ready for to do with them afterwards. This way, once they know how to wash and dry their own clothes there will be no question what to do with them afterwards. Be sure and teach them how to be responsible with the iron lest your house be burned down.

Teach them to do these things so that it becomes a part of them. I don't care if you are well off enough to have a maid. Do it. Otherwise you will have children whom can't take care of themselves and will grow up expecting someone to do everything for them. Don't make them your slaves but do not raise helpless children either.

Make sure they can't do the things they enjoy without first having done their chores. If they know they can't do the things they enjoy without having taken care of their responsibilities then they will usually want to get them out of the way instead of putting them off. Yes, they will try to get out of it or half do them sometimes. Be firm. No fun until it is done and done right.

Do not wait too late to do this. If you wait until the child is say 13 years old to do this, you are going to have major problems. The child wasn't expected to do any of this before and will wonder why all of sudden "why now" and you kind of sort of can't blame them. It will be a steep uphill fight as they will be set in their ways, so don't let it happen. Seven and eight years of age are ok to start, but any three to four year old can swing a broom and push a vacuum cleaner. Generally speaking they will want to do it on their own after seeing you do it and try to do it without you asking. Encourage it. Don't stop them. If they want to help, welcome it no matter what it is. If you don't you will one day miss and regret it. Don't worry that they may be too young to handle it. Explain and teach as you go. Make them think they are doing something even if it's too much for them to handle. Do not turn them away no matter what. One day they will be able to handle it and you may want or need the help and it won't hurt that they already know or have a good idea of what to do making your job easier. Besides, it's good quality time between you and your child. You want all the quality time with your child you can get. Do not discriminate between male and female children. There are girls that can hang in there with the toughest boys. Make sure they know they are girls and want to be girls but that is no reason they can't be allowed to do what a boy can. If they can handle it, they can handle it. Trust me, better to have a tough girly girl whom is pretty than a soft sorry one that can't do anything except sit around and look pretty and one day when you really need her can't do or won't do squat even to save her own life.

Chapter Twenty-One
Your Children's Friends

Be very, very aware of who your child's friends are and whom they are hanging around with. You want to meet their friends and parents early and find out what they and their friends are like. If you don't, the friend or friends could be a very bad influence on your child. Don't discriminate against a child because say you're a Baptist and they are Methodist for instance. But you want to make sure your child won't get a whole bunch of bad idea's such as all of a sudden its ok to disrespect you, vandalize others property, steal, curse, etc. Your child could be very impressionable so you have to be on guard for such issues. Eventually, the other child will want to hang out with your child at your place and or vice versa making the parent meeting all the more important. Be sure of the environment your child is going into before this happens. Otherwise, if you don't like the situation and say no you are going to look like the bad guy so get this out of the way early before it can become an issue. Your child may go into their friend's home while playing outside without a thought so you must be on top of this issue without seeming overly protective. It only takes a moment for something to happen to a child so be sure you are in control of where they go and with whom they play.

Notes

Chapter Twenty-Two
Your Child's Dreams and Ideas

A t some point always make sure you make time to listen to your children. Encourage them to tell you what is on their minds. Encourage them to have dreams and ideas no matter how far out, (within reason of course, I don't have to tell you what to do if those ideas involve hurting others for instance), and wild. They could be the next inventor of something positive or great or someone whom may take humanity to new levels if they can only get the chances.

Get them early on into music, gymnastics, dance, acting, and ballet, whatever their talents may be. Don't let it pass them by. It will add to their development. Don't limit them. Just because you didn't get to do those things don't stop them.

Take them places they've never been before. It will expand their minds. Expose them to nature and science. Give them experiences they will not have hanging around their neighborhoods. In so doing you will expand their world and thus world view. Small minds think of and conceive small minded things.

Note: No matter the age, always teach your children the difference between fantasy and reality as well as practicality and materialism. Children have a thirst for knowledge and answers to their questions. If you are unwilling to satisfy those needs, they will look elsewhere and possibly confide in others who do not have their best interest at heart. Always be honest, open to listen and answer their questions no matter what. If you don't, your child may develop unhealthy goals, dreams and ideas that you will not be happy with based off of fantasy and material desires. You must set the real life example for them to follow for they see and watch you every day. Given this, you must always live that which you say and preach to them at all times.

Notes

Chapter Twenty-Three
Clothes and Shoes

Choose your children's clothing and shoes with some consideration for their desires. However, do it analytically and smartly as a child will ever rarely do so. Besides, they need to be appreciative. You're the one spending the money, not them.

Dress your children modestly and tastefully from the beginning and tell everyone who tells you to dress them with the times to go do something with themselves. What do I mean? It's becoming fashionable to dress children as though they are adults. But they are not adults. They are children. Some of the stars for instance let their 3 and 4 year old girls wear high heels and tight revealing pants and dress that are a bit short. There is gangsta wear for boys. I don't know about you but I wouldn't and as a matter of fact so long as I have had anything do with it have not allowed my children to wear such clothing. The result, my daughter is modest and not interested in looking other than she should and my son isn't interested in wearing his pants hanging off his butt nor looking like a hook.

On the subject of dresses, no splits and dresses should be to or just above the knees. When they bend over no one should be able to see anything. As a matter of fact particularly when they wear a dress to school have them wear some shorts under there. You want to do this as young girls do not know any better when playing and jumping around with everything showing nor do you want them to be an easy target for predators. Don't dress them in revealing V necks either. The moment they start getting some upper development get them a starter bra or else they will go into the outside world with something poking. Need help, enlist the help of a female you trust if the mother is not available or not a good source of help as you need to make sure whatever bra your daughter wears are becoming of a young girl. That is more important than you think. If and when you have to take your young girl to buy a bra you will be shocked at what's available. I think someone let a fox into the hen house when it comes to children's clothing because there is stuff out there for children I never thought I would see and should not be but I digress. Let's just say I'm starting to wonder if there is a conspiracy to make our daughters look like young sluts and our sons look like young hooks. It is as though someone wants to make them morally desensitized at a very young age. If so I don't like that plan and neither should you. We vote for what kind of clothing will be available to our children and ultimately us as well with our pocket books whether we realize it or not. So vote on the clothes available to youth, yourself, and other things for that matter with your pocket book. Make sure you cast that vote, not your child.

Just because it's the in thing now and a lot of others are doing it does not mean it is to be done. They should look nice and like what they are wearing but make damn sure it is appropriate be damned the current fashion and what others do and may say.

On the issue of shoes, be sure they are durable and comfortable as well as appropriate to you and for what they will be used for. Let the child first choose the shoes they like and then out of that set of choices determine the ones you like based on your set criteria. You must have the last word and determination. Children often make choices based on what their friends are wearing or what they think is in fashion. They are not thinking about how good the shoe is going to feel on their feet when they do whatever they are going to do in them even if that is just walking around in them. They are not considering whether or not their shoes will hold up for a while or fall apart in two weeks. Those thoughts never enter their young minds. Boys can be especially hard on shoes. Children must be taught early regarding shoes that how good the shoe looks is less important than how it feels and how durable they are. Bad shoes can damage your children's feet and cause problems that a doctor, and you and your pocket book, will later have to deal with. Also, do you really want to spend $70 and up on a pair of shoes just because it has a bunch of cool whatever on them to get the attention of young eyes that at most, the child may wear for 6 months maybe 7 tops? What I had to do with my daughter for instance is buy the shoes she wanted and the ones I knew she needed. The ones she wanted were the ones she thought looked good because of friends. The ones I wanted her to have looked ok and were nice to her but were not the style she felt she wanted. Later, begrudgingly, she had to admit the ones I wanted her to have were the best ones. The ones that were her first choice hurt her feet after awhile. This later led her to ask me why it is the less in style ones are always so comfortable and feel so good while the in style ones tend to hurt and don't last long. I explained to her regarding so called in style shoes the manufacturer knows the shoes they make and why you buy them and thus cater to that want with not much regard to other things such as the comfort and care of your feet. The other shoes they know are being chosen with the comfort and well being of the feet first and thus that is focused on more than the looks though the looks are still important to them. I then proceeded to explain to her what happens when you mistreat your feet and explained what happens when a foot doctor must work on your feet. You may have to have the same talk with your children.

Regarding the cleaning of tennis shoes, do not; I repeat do not put shoes in the washing machine! That is a great way to ruin them. Buy a small brush just for that purpose. When your child messes up their shoes, you will need that brush and some soap that is without color and powerful scents. You can then wash the shoes in the tub or sink. Do not use a sink used for washing dishes! First remove the shoestrings. They should be cleaned separately from the shoes. Dampen the shoes with cold or luke warm running water. Soap up the brushes bristles. Now scrub the shoes clean starting with the inside of them first and saving the bottom of the shoes for last. Once done completely rinse the shoes of all soap and debris and place them on top of your dryer so that they may dry. Anytime they become dirty enough do this. They will almost look like new. Be sure and make your child watch you do this. Then the next time walk them through doing it. Soon they will be able to do it without your help. Naturally you don't expect a 2 year old to do this but once the child is mature enough they can say maybe 4 years old. Never underestimate what a child can, do just because of their age. They often just need good guidance. Besides, once the child becomes responsible for cleaning up their own shoes and not you, they will become mindful of messing them up.

There are a lot of other numerous tips like this one I could mention that probably deserve their own book.

Notes

Chapter Twenty-Four
Hygiene

Teach your children to brush their teeth after every meal unless they are out and about and of course can't do that. In that case, they should understand that once they get home they are to brush their teeth then unless they are about to eat after they arrive. Make sure that you teach them not only how to properly brush their teeth but also how to properly rinse and gargle. After the first rinse they should gargle twice then rinse one last time. This may not seem important but children will want to rush through that last part or not even do it at all. I know. Yuk. But they do it. Teach them to floss as well.

Teach your children to take a shower every night. I deliberately said shower and not bath. Children have a tendency to play with the soap in the tub. So now you have soapy water mixed with dirt if they went on ahead and bathed. If they take a bath chances are some of that will just be left on their skin. Nix it from the beginning. They shower all of that comes off rather than sitting in a pool of it. Be sure and teach them how to properly bathe. There's nothing like your child coming out of the restroom claiming they took a good bath or shower and yet they're under arms reek. To that end, make sure they regularly wash their hair. Boys should wash their hair every time they bathe. Girls should do so almost as much if not just as much. Believe it or not, just the act of washing the hair with a non scented soap or shampoo can help with sinus problems. Think about it. All day you are going about your business, your scalp is sweating and shedding skin flakes and your hair is gathering dust and other pollutants in the air. Then you carry that with you everywhere you go and unbeknownst to you, you may actually be breathing it. Not to mention some of that goes into your pillow every time you lay your head on it without having washed your hair. If you wash your hair before going to sleep every night you will discover you breathe and sleep better and so the same will your children if you enforce this rule. Besides, you should make sure that the idea of jumping into bed without a bath/shower and washing of the hair is repulsive.

Teach your children to wash their feet when they get home. Yes, you should be doing the same thing as well. Your feet have been sweating in their shoes all day and they have foot odor. Before you and or they relax and put your feet on the couch and or what have you they should be washed and clean lest you spread this to these various objects. There's nothing like sitting down where your child or other family just left and smelling their own personal toe Jam.

If your child has been out playing or at school all day, be sure and make it known to them they are not to sit and or lay down on the couch without getting out of the clothes they have been wearing and then bathing themselves. If you and they do not follow this rule you will discover that your furniture stinks and is unpleasant to frankly have anything to do with. It will also take on a grungy appearance. How often do you want to purchase new furniture or have it cleaned? You may hear me say this many times. There is no better smell than clean. Clean does not bother you in any form or fashion. Clean is just clean.

Chapter Twenty-Five
Make Up, Perfume and Ear Rings

O n the issue of makeup, do as you wish but I am telling you to keep the makeup away from your daughter until she can buy her own. Does that sound harsh? Let me explain. Young girls need to learn that they were provided with beauty when they were born by the Creator, you and their mother. Beauty does not come out of a bottle, the tip of a brush or a can. You must be beautiful inside first and it must emanate from your mind. Besides, what does a young girl need with it anyway? Who is she wearing it for? It should not even be on her mind. **She is a child** and should be focused on being a child. She goes out to play, plays inside and goes to school. That's it. If she's doing something else other than that there is a problem and you'd better take care of it now right away. Girls should be taught to be themselves and not try to look like others. Once they know they are beautiful without trying to look like others it will do wonders for their self-esteem. Keep images away from them that convince them they have to have all of that gobble de gook just to look nice and presentable for subconsciously they are learning they have to buy and have that stuff to look like anything and or be noticed. In doing so they may attract the wrong attention. Also, make up tends to be loaded with very unpleasant chemicals and even heavy metals. For instance, did you know that certain eye shadows contain arsenic? Do your own personal research on the chemicals in these various cosmetics and even the soap and toothpaste you use for that matter and I believe you will be very surprised and probably even taken aback by it. Personally, I only use natural hygiene products and no cosmetics and have taught my children the same. Now, on the issue of perfumes and colognes, don't let boys and girls experiment with these until they are well into their teens and even then carefully monitor the usage of them. Don't let them walk out the door smelling like they poured the whole bottle on themselves. It's not good for them and no one should have to be forced to smell it no matter how good they think they smell and this should be explained and taught to them. Many people have allergy problems and these various concoctions to make one smell good set them off. Besides, once again, whom are they wearing this stuff for? **They are still children and you go to school to learn.** Frankly, the best smell in the world to me is clean. Make sure they are not using these various scents to cover up neglect of hygiene. There's nothing worse than the combination of perfume or cologne and the pungent smell of body odor due to lack of proper hygiene. On the issue of earrings, I know its customary to have a girls ears pierced when they are young, however, my suggestion is it would be far better to just say no and if they ask to wear such give them some clip on earrings. Why? Because they tend to get infected and can get ripped off while playing. That hurts. Also, there are a lot of nerves passing through the ear lobes. It's not talked about much or not widely known, but earrings have at times been found to be the cause of chronic pains that seem like they should have nothing do with the simple piercing of the ears and placement of ear rings in them. But when they were removed and the ear lobes allowed to heal the problems went away. Once again, I know there are going to be lots of people whom will disagree with me but do please consider what I am saying. They should be of age where they can make the decision whether or not to have their ears pierced without outside influences. Keep in mind, maturity should be a significant part in their decision. On the issue of boys wearing earrings just say no. Period. It just isn't becoming of a young man to be wearing earrings.

On the issue of girls and boys putting earrings in various places too numerous to mention only limited by their imaginations, just say no. Not on your watch. If they want to do **it** when they become adults so be it but not as long as you have something to do with it. Once again, **they are children.** What in the world are they doing even considering such options and where or who are they getting such ideas from? There are a lot of downsides to one's health and otherwise to getting these things placed all over the body. For instance, like when they are old enough to get a job and have to go before an interviewer.

Chapter Twenty-Six
Love and Affection

Make sure your children know that you love them but do so in your actions as well as words. Tell them you love them and then prove it. Hug them and what have you in reason. Play with and tickle them. Just be mindful to tone it down, as they get older. As they get older some things are no longer appropriate as they were when they were younger so be mindful. No matter how old they get they are still your babies but you must be able to let go and recognize that they get older and mature so be aware.

So past affection what is love? Is it buying them lots of material things? No. Buying them everything they want is buying their affection. Not loving them. Neither is letting them have their way all the time and or allowing them to run over you. Love is shown in the care and disciple you give them, teaching them right from wrong and steering them on the right path to becoming upstanding citizens whom are a benefit to the society we live in. Love is in listening to them and their ideas, concerns and questions. Love is in the quality time you spend with them. Taking them to the museum, planetarium, park, beach, a dam, waterfall, amusement park, water park, racetrack, nature tour, whatever you can think of. Love is not only protecting them but also protecting them from themselves. Love is making sure they go to good schools instead of just any school. Love is making sure they are well and if they get sick not getting mad when they throw up on you. Love is teaching them to be clean, neat, responsible, and to have the initiative to do positive things on their own. Love is teaching them how to build, repair and also cook things instead of depending on others to do it for them, (within reason of course). Love is teaching them how to deal with others and the outside world. Love is teaching them how to handle their money and understand the value of it.

Love is teaching them to be appreciative of what they have. Love is teaching them to love themselves and thus be able to love others. This can go on and on but by now you should catch my drift and understand where I'm going with this.

Special Note:

Do not be over protective. Yes, you must be firm and keep them on the right path, however, if you smother them and they never ever have breathing room to develop social skills of their own, your child will develop social problems and may grow up to be a social problem themselves. Be loving but not overly so. Remember, keep everything in balance and allow them room to grow and develop. After all, do you really want to do all of their thinking and feeling for them all of your lives? Teenagers can be rebellious enough as it is. Don't give them an honest justification to be so.

Chapter Twenty-Seven
Your Child going to School

Before your child is old enough to go to school, you must give serious consideration to where they are going to go to school. In a perfect world you live in a neighborhood that has the perfect elementary school, middle school and high school. Unfortunately, we don't live in a perfect world. Maybe you can't move into that neighborhood even should it exist. If you are lucky you live in a neighborhood with at least one of these. If not you better learn fast how to get your child transferred and riding the bus.

I learned the hard way. My son benefited from what I learned trying to get his older sister into various schools. I started off not knowing what to do but was determined and learned quickly. You will have to as well as the schools do not make it easy.

Not everyone can send his or her child to a private school and even then you don't always get what you think you are paying for. Look seriously at magnet programs. Look at charter schools also, but very cautiously. Some are good and some are bad. As in all things you must do your homework and seriously look at the school you are considering. All school districts usually have info sheets on their schools that tell you how they are rated, demographics of both teachers and students, and the programs the school offers. Seriously look at that information. Also, visit the school and seriously check it out for yourself. See what the students and teachers are like if you can. If you like it, take your child there and let them see it. If the school is right then enroll your child there.

My advice is to assess the situation long before your child is old enough to go to school. You don't want to be a hostage to zoning. It can make the difference between a good school and or the school from hell. Find out about all the possible schools and check them out. Then go to the top 3 you'd want your child to go through and find out what it takes to get them in. Mind you, do this one or two years before you will have to worry about it. You don't want to later say, "Damn, if only I had known and put my child there." It's a bad feeling.

If you can't transfer your child to a better school, you better make plans to move somewhere with decent schools quick before it's too late. If not, I hope you can afford private school or can find a decent charter school that really teaches. Some charter schools are really good but there are a lot of bad ones out there so beware and do your homework on them.

Regarding teachers, even in the best of schools you can have a bad teacher so always get to know your child's teacher. You need to do this for two reasons. One you want to make sure the teacher is good but reason number two is that if your child tries to say that teacher is no good or what have you, you can get to the bottom of the situation quickly. Just because your child says something is wrong with a teacher doesn't make it true so hold up before you confront that teacher. It could be that your child doesn't like the teacher because they make them do their work and use their brain. Maybe the child got in trouble for something they did and doesn't like the fact they can't get away with things like their friends in other teachers' classrooms. Find out what is really going on because the problem may really be your child and not the teacher. Only once, or twice did I have an issue where the problem was the teacher. All the other times it was my child. Children whom know that you are not going to leap to their defense but instead investigate the situation will be less likely to get themselves into situations. That makes your job easier because in that case, you can better figure out if a teacher really is a problem as some nut jobs do sometimes manage to get through the cracks in which case you don't want your child to become a victim. Hence, listen very carefully to what your child says, as no one knows them better than you then listen to the teacher very carefully. Afterwards, combine the facts and look for discrepancies with either of them and or both.

Occasionally your child will have the misfortune of getting a bad teacher who is mean and/or just has it in for them, etc. Once you know this to truly be the case, be ready to get your child out of that teacher's class whatever it takes. Whatever you do, don't get into a confrontation with said teacher lest you look like the bad guy to the administration of the school. Be warned, teachers gossip and talk. Be careful that you don't receive a negative label attached to your child thus affecting their education.

Past that, be on top of what your child is doing in school. You don't want to be blindsided by a report card of bad grades. Some children naturally want to excel while others must be pushed. You must get the need to be pushed child to understand that it is their responsibility to make good grades and improve themselves and no one else's for you cannot hold their hands all of their lives. They must want to do it on their own. If not it is a hard cold world out there awaiting them and they must be made aware of that.

By the way, make sure your child goes to bed at a decent time. It helps with growth as it has been found that children grow at night during deep sleep. Yes, I know I've already mentioned this but I can't stress it enough. A sleepy child doesn't function very well in school and may be a child with behavioral problems. Make them go to bed at night and get the recommended amount of sleep. Don't let them develop the habit of using homework as an excuse to stay up. When they get home, they should go on ahead and get their homework out of the way. You also must teach them to get themselves up in the morning that they may be on time to school. If you don't, they can ruin the day. Think having to go to the school to answer why your child is late and having to answer to your job why you are late if they're lateness is making you late.

Important: If you can, set up a separate bank account for your child that is to never ever be touched. Add to it constantly and consistently. College is expensive. Your child is not guaranteed a scholarship or grant. Things presently are hard and appear to be getting harder. School loans seem to just as bad as buying a home. Make this account their college fund. I don't know what college will cost by the time your child reaches school but based on the way things are going presently I hope I am wrong but, it undoubtedly will be more expensive than it is now. Even if they are able to get scholarships and grants they still may not be enough, however, every little bit counts. Try not to let high school come upon you and find yourself wondering what you are going to do as the college years march closer and closer to you. Some high schools get your child ready for college and may even offer college courses including and up to giving the opportunity to acquire an associate's degree at graduation. I wish that had been available to me when I was in school.

Notes

Chapter Twenty-Eight
Sex, Drugs and Crime

No. I'm not touching on this too soon. Children these days have some idea of what sex is and in some cases know what drugs are even at the young age of five years old. I am not making this up. Thanks to TV, movies, the internet and just overhearing the conversation of or accidentally stumbling onto their parents in the act, they often have a surprising amount of knowledge as to what sex is, however inaccurate or convoluted due to immaturity it may be. Do not go mute on them. The moment you find out your child knows or thinks they know something it is time to have a serious talk with them based on their maturity level and what they have the ability to understand at the age they are at. Do not have a talk with a male child you would not with a female one and vice versa. Clear up any bad information and explain what reproduction is and how it works based on their age. If you don't it does not take away their curiosity to find out and you don't want them to run into someone who will be obliged to help them find out whether that person or persons be someone their own age or an teenage or adult predator. Tell them what they need to know, (I said tell them, no demonstrations please), and usually the curiosity is taken care of and goes away. However, along with that knowledge include a healthy dose of what will happen if they go out there and try to experience sex.

That means tell them the hard nitty gritty and even terrifying truth's about STD's, the changes that will happen in their bodies as a result of engaging in such acts to young, the reputation they will get particularly if they are a girl and last but no less important, pregnancy. To my knowledge the youngest girl to get pregnant was 9 years old. Can you imagine your 9-year-old little girl being a mother or your 9-year-old little boy being a father? I'm not making this up. One thing you can do for the girls that will scare them straight is get a film/movie showing what a woman goes through being pregnant all the way up through labor and birth. That alone is enough to scare the crap out of most girls and should be required viewing for all teenage girls I think. Teach and make clear to them the consequences and what it will do to their lives. Once it happens, their life is changed forever. They will no longer be able to do what their friends do and babies are not cute little dolls. They need to know that.

The boys need to get the same lesson with the caveat that that child is their flesh and blood as well and they should be responsible if they do it and it should not be all the responsibility of the girl. Yes, I know its presently is ending up that way usually but don't teach your son that. If he has a sense of responsibility instead of it's her problem if it happens he will be less likely to do it. By the way, boys are always getting most of the blame but there had to be a girl out their wanting, willing and waiting to open her legs to let a boy get her pregnant. It does take two to tangle you know. Teach abstinence but don't rely on it. Do be prepared to teach safe sex if asked and it becomes necessary to do so.

Now then, on the subject of drugs, at a young age teach your child how bad it is to abuse and use drugs and what it does to the human body and thus them if they should be stupid enough to do it. When I was in Junior High School, they played a movie that showed people using drugs. It showed them taking the drugs, what they looked like after they took the drugs, what they looked like once the high wore off and the effects of that. It showed them talking about how they will do anything such as lie, cheat, steal, sell their own bodies to anyone and even kill to get more drugs and get that high back. It showed real people who were really on drugs become so consumed with the drugs they didn't care how they looked. You got to actually hear them narrate how they wish they had never gotten hooked on drugs and how the drug consummation was wrecking or had wrecked their lives and how hard it is to get off of the drugs they were taking. Then it showed real drug addicts overdosing from trying to get that higher high. It was very gross but they showed it uncensored in all its glory. Some of them went unconscious right before your eyes. Then they showed some of them die from the overdose and how these people were often found in alley ways, dumpsters, abandoned homes or even their own home and how they had to have proper burials even if no family ever showed or was present. Then they showed the drug addicts that sought help and what they had to go through. By go through I mean the withdrawal. You got to see them lose total control of their bodies in withdrawal. No one talked while this movie was on. I don't remember what the name of this movie was but I can think of a few good titles. I have gone looking for this movie but haven't been able to find it. I know there are going to be people who will protest against it but that movie needs to be found and shown in every school to every child. It will scare them straight because any one child who sees it should ask the following question. Why in the world in my right mind would I want to do that to myself?

Also, on the subject of smoking and drinking, it should be explained to children that smoking and drinking are nothing more than legalized drugs. Just because it is legal doesn't mean it's ok to do. This should be abundantly clear as many of them can't wait till they are old enough to drink and smoke thinking it will somehow make them look cool, more grown up and adult. It should be explained that all they are doing is paying someone to kill them. Yes, it's a slow death but it is death all the same. Teach your children not to associate with others whom use drugs even if they are family members. Teach them to never date nor want such people. Also, explain that if they ever decide to deal drugs there is a jail or prison cell that will be waiting for them somewhere. Maybe not tomorrow but eventually it will happen. We have to get it through to our children as long as there is a demand for illicit drugs there will be illicit drug usage. Treating the problem through the penal system will never get rid of it. You can fill the nation's prisons to the brim, but as long as there is a demand for illicit drugs, the problem will never ever go away. No one will continue to sell anything they can't actually make a profit from.

If you have really very good reason to suspect that your child is doing drugs of any kind, just doing a spot check of their room is not enough. Your child may be smart enough to make sure nothing of the sort can be found in their room. That first spot check will also make them aware that you are on to them and they will just double their efforts not to get caught by you. Heaven forbid, you might need to get them tested. If you do and they are on drugs, be prepared to put them in rehab and get them off of the drugs they are addicted to. Then do some soul searching as to how in the world did this happen. Was it their friends, your environment, etc? Whatever it is figure it out and change it so that it does not happen again.

Now, on the subject of kids and crime, this goes back to morals. You should have nipped this in the bud early teaching them not to do wrong and that if they are bored there are better things to do rather than vandalize or take what belongs to others and bullying does not make you better nor stronger than someone else. However, there are always influences out there and maybe your kid gets involved with the wrong kid or kids despite your best efforts. If you have done everything you can it's time for some more drastic measures. Find out about juveniles who died doing crime and show them the list. See if you can take them to a juvenile detention facility and show them all the hard asses that are there and ask them would they like to end up there. There use to be programs where a child could spend a day in a cell away from people that had actually done crimes under constant supervision so that they could see what if feels like to actually be in jail. They use to show this on TV when I was a kid. They need to bring it back and make problem children experience it. You also might want to consider showing them what an actual prison looks like. There's nothing like having a metal gate slam behind you and not being able to get out without a prison guard letting you out, not to mention seeing all of those prison guards in guard towers waiting to put a bullet in anyone whom tries to escape. Certain cable stations use to have a show where they showed all of the realities of being in prison right down to the rapes. They had a man named Stan the Syrup Man. Stan the Syrup Man explained that when a new inmate came in he would break them in by putting syrup in his ass, (I am not making this up), make the new inmate eat it out with his eyes open so that he could not fantasize that he was doing it with a woman but with a man. If that doesn't scare you straight I don't know what will. National geographic recently had a series on women's prisons. Wow, they are even more violent and vicious than the men. Girls need to see that. I wonder if they have a Susie the Syrup Woman. Either way, these need to be mandatory viewing for children whom are going down that road. They need to know if they are hanging with the wrong crowd they can become victims of guilty by association. Girl or boy, if they are hanging with hooks and happen to be around when the hooks get busted, the cops are going to assume they are hooks too and bust them as well. As a last resort, threaten to send them to boot camp and then if they force you to, follow through.

If your child is in danger of falling into the crime scene and or drug trap make sure they are more scared of what you will do to them when they get out of detention, jail, prison, etc, than what will happen if they go into such institutions for doing crime. According to one of my best friends, he had a friend that dealt drugs whom wanted him to join him. My friend refused, as he was terrified of his grandmother and what she would do if she found out about it let alone what she'd do to him once he finished doing time if he got caught. The friend's mother did not instill such threats into him. That friend of his was eventually caught and to this day is still in the federal penitentiary. If I remember correctly that friend is going to get out somewhere around 2020. He's been in there since the 1980's. When you are in federal there is neither early release nor probation. You are in there for the duration of the time meted out to you. These things need to be explained to wannabe hard assess. Once you are in prison no one except your family cares what happens to you and at night you can hear the screams of those who get raped.

NOTE:

While we're on this subject, does your son like to walk around with his pants hanging off his butt? Explain to him that the practice originated in prison. You see, when an inmate wants other inmates to know he's ready to get poked in the you know what, he wears his pants baggy. That's the signal. Then ask your son if he's ready to get poked by someone. If he's not too far gone usually they pull their britches up. He needs to know this so that he knows it's not cool. For the life of me I don't understand how that became cool. How does looking like you don't know how to wear pants, holding them in your hands as you walk, showing your underwear make you look like anything other than afool! Young girls should be taught that boys who wear their pants this way are gross not cool and it should be done by both parents early so that it takes hold in their psyches before their peers can influence them.

*Actually, girls determine and cause this kind of behavior to go on. Think about it for a moment. Boys generally do a lot of this stuff to get the attention of girls and thus a girl or girls.! If the majority of girls refused to have anything to do with boys whom engage in such behavior and wore their clothes in such uncouth ways, how long do you think it would be before we saw a significant curtailment in these behaviors? **Nothing happens in a vacuum. There is a reason for everything.***

By the way, the number of young ladies going to jail and prison is rising. Girls get rapped and beat up in penal institutions to. All things considered, the same I just mentioned for boys should be part and par for girls.

Notes

Where's My Med's?

And so you fell under her spell and decided to take up that hayride with her. Up and down and around and around you bounced with her in the wagon. Oh what merry fun and such a wonderful feeling it was. It was so fine and sweet you wished it would last forever. Then as they always do, things change as they in exorbitantly do, the ride developed some bumps along the way you never knew. Then with a pop you discovered little passengers, whew. It was then she told you that you are captain of all old and new. In the back of your mind you thought, "Hey, I'm not sure I like this maybe I should bail while I can", but it was too late and yes she already knew. To calm you down she said, "It will be alright, you are in command. We just need your guidance we shall fatefully follow you just keep us on the straight path all will be swell", she said to you with a fateful yet knowing smile and gleam in the eye that made you wonder if you only knew. For sure enough as the ride progressed thine little passengers grew. As they grew they brought forth their own little minds that often went frightfully askew. And so when you were contemplating the road they often interjected that they wanted to take the reins too. And as you matched wits with them to keep them in line the horses looked back fearfully yet expectantly as they knew, if you didn't man up and put those little minds in check there may be a wreck taking them into it too. Just when things seemed to be straight your trusty mate decided she'd make a play for the reigns too. A new battle then ensued, now what do you do? You put her in her place too. After all, it took two to tangle and get into this wild ride,· it wasn't just you alone doing the do. Now your hair is getting prematurely gray as this ride is no longer just a ride. Besides steering the horses around the dips and bumps along the way, and protecting the young minds from the wolves beckoning from the sides of the road, you now have to protect and indeed fight to protect them from themselves. As they fight to do all that is contrary to a safe way down this road, yet keep the first mate from excerpting all you do.

Wouldn't it have been great if you had had that wagon to yourself in the first place instead? For then you could've done some better screening and gotten a much more loyal first mate, damn it where's the road back to the starting point, it's been covered from your view so you must keep going as best you can instead.

Where's my med's?

Chapter Twenty-Nine
You have Discovered that You are Really or are soon to be a Single Parent even though You are actually With the Children's Mother

D epending on what stage of a relationship you are in with your child or children's mother, everything I have gone over in this book still applies with the caveat that you can't include the mother in the equation any longer. For instance, what if she is hurt so that she cannot do anything anymore or worst, she is no longer in this life. You still must carry on and your child or children do not just disappear. On the other hand, if you are still with the mother, but she is not doing any positive mothering, you must function as though she didn't exist, as you must do all of the rearing, caring, loving, etc without her even though you still live with her. Some women just aren't very good mothers and God Bless you positively if you have had the misfortune of finding out after getting with her and having children by her. If you are divorced from the mother and have custody the same applies.

Just because you are a man does not mean you can't be a loving parent to your children and take care of them just as well as a woman. Society thinks that but you do not have to ascribe to that. So don't. Your children are depending on you. They have no one else more qualified than you the father. The mother was supposed to be qualified and half of the children's complete make up came from her. The other half the children's complete make up comes from you so why would you not be just as qualified. If you can make them you can take care of them just like a woman is supposed to. It will be harder though because women have all sorts of support mechanisms in place to help them, which are absent for men, hence the reason I told you to prepare from the very beginning. I said harder, not impossible. It is being done every day by fathers who have custody of their children.

A bad mother is less pronounced because of these various factors not to mention how others are more ready to help her than you just because of that implement swinging between your legs. But that is no cause to give up and give in and thus throw away the lives of your children. You must rise to the occasion no matter what so do it and do not put the responsibility on others.

Like I said before, the children didn't ask to be here and they cannot fend for themselves. This is your seed we are talking about. If you need help ok get it, but do not fling them to the winds nor depend on others to raise your children.

The jails and prisons of this land are littered with people whom did not have the strong hand of their fathers to guide them. For the women whom are going to gripe they came up and were raised just by their mothers and/or are raising children just fine by themselves, GREAT! You go ladies. But your reality is not the only reality and there are plenty of adults raised in single mother households who came out ok but will tell you they wish they had had the guidance of their fathers and or wish they could have learned from their fathers what only a father can impart. Then, there is a bunch that did not come out ok and their examples are very numerous. You can see them on the streets, our schools, and juvenile detention. It is said that a whole generation is being lost and going down the tubes as I type this.

As I was saying, it's all up to you. Just do it. Your children will love you for it. You may find that you will have to draw up plans to acquire custody of your children and get away from the mother. Why? Because if she is of no help or worst negating everything you are trying to teach your children with bad habits whether intentional or not, this causes confusion in the children and will only hurt them.

Getting away may be hard to do though, whether you still want to be with her or not. If you love her and want to stick it out and try to work it out ok. Get some counseling that both of you can go to together. But it may not turn out the way you want. She has to want to change. You can't make her change and forget that in time she will mature bull crap. If she doesn't genuinely want to it will never happen and you will be deluding yourself. If and when you decide enough is enough and want to leave formulate how you are going to acquire custody and take care of the children by yourself quietly without her knowledge as the court may favor the woman. Ideally, try to reason with her that you are the better parent and that the children should go with you. Realize, however, that is ideally. This only works if she is reasonable. It's rare, no matter how bad a mother is, that she will willingly give up the children even though she may know you are the better parent. There is a whole industry waiting to help her sock it to you so the last thing you want to do is give her any information she can use against you, including the fact you've had enough and now just want to take care of your kids without her and whatever negatives she may be contributing to the situation. She can be the worst mother known to mankind and many courts will give the kids to her unless she walks into court openly doing drugs in front of the judge so you'd better get your case together without her knowing it. Child support workers actually get bonuses for socking it to you. That's a little known fact they don't want people to know about. By all means, once you know that the situation between you and the mother is coming to a head, seek the services of a good attorney whom will be on your side.

To that end, make yourself abreast of what age your state will allow your children to choose which parent they want to live with. If you are close to that age for them you may want to bid your time and let them choose.

Please, if you are an abusive, bad, sorry excuse for a father (DEAD BEAT DAD), do not do this and let the kids go to the best parent. But then if that were you, would you care enough to be reading this book?

There are various organizations that can help you. Check them out. Find out your avenues and then carefully, quietly and methodically prepare for a fight.

You see, even if the woman doesn't want to take care of the children she usually will not want to let them go because then she has to admit to herself and others that she sucks as a parent. She will not want to do that. Also, women will use the children against you for you not wanting to deal with them anymore. Don't give her the opportunity to do that. The children are living, breathing, feeling human beings. They are neither commodities nor a club to hit fathers, (such as yourself), over the head with. Not all women are like this but many of them are. They will not care about how it affects and or hurts your children as long as they can use them to get at and hurt you. So plan how to keep it from happening. Your children do not deserve this. Document everything, what you do, what she does and or any lack thereof. You will need it. Keep documents safe and hidden. It could take time. In Texas once the child is 12 the child can determine on their own which parent they wish to live with. It varies from state to state though and is subject to change. You will have to research the area you live in to find out.

Whatever you do, keep your cool. Some women may hit and or do various mean things towards you out of spite. Sometimes they do this because they want you to strike back so that they can have something to use against you or damage your good character. Do not do it. No matter what she does don't stoop to her level. If you do, she may call the authorities causing you to acquire a bad record. Chances are great that no one will believe you when you say you reacted in self-defense. If she's being violent, the best thing to do is let her do something incriminating to herself and then you can call the authorities on her particularly if she has wounded you. Keep in mind, I'm not telling you to just sit there and allow her to break your limbs and or kill you. However, when the authorities show up at your call, (not hers!), and see that you've inflicted no harm whatsoever to her and are instead calm and she's the one doing things, particularly if she puts any marks on you, usually it will be her that gets taken away. I said usually. I can't guarantee that the authorities are going to be reasonable. But you have a much better chance if she's the one whom is obviously a nut case. Not you. If that happens, you've got a very good piece of solid evidence to show how you are a better parent than her as it is now public evidence. I promise you if it's the other way around such will be used against you.

This chapter is why I said everything in the beginning. You want to make damn sure you do not end up in this position. It's like being a prisoner in a prison without bars and walls. Your children will be like unwitting hostages keeping you in that prison.

Yes, you can leave but what happens to your children if you leave without them? You may have just doomed them to a lot of suffering. A lot of women, if mad at the father, will take their anger and frustrations out on the children as the father is not around to receive it and the children can't defend themselves from such abuse as an adult male can. It doesn't matter that it's not right. It's what they do. The child will not know nor understand why they are being mistreated. Only that they are and can't do anything about it. The mother will also try to fill their heads up with all kinds of lies and half truths about you defaming your character in order to turn them to her side at your expense. You can end up with a child whom hates your guts yet can't explain why they hate your guts as they have no good reason other than what the mother said. You are their defender and if you leave without them they are vulnerable. A woman can and often will turn your children into a political football or club to use either to get you back or against you. You don't want this to happen as who will really be hurt and damaged by this are the children. (By the way, I should not have to tell you not to engage in such behavior should I? Don't render evil for evil. It will only make you look bad and convict you in your own soul. Do protect yourself though.)

Yes, you will be hurt as well. That's the point. A woman will not care whom she hurts, even if they are her children. So long as she can get at you she will do it. Not all women are this way but a significant majority of them are. So do your best not to put yourself nor leave your children in such a position. That is why I began this book as I did and yes this paragraph is a repeat of some idea's I may have just said as I feel it is very important.

Once you are locked into a situation like this you are in for a good long while until you can remedy it. In the meantime, the stress you will encounter in this shituation, (no, that wasn't a typo), as described will affect upon you a slow death. It won't matter how good your health is, stress will give you all kinds of health problems you never thought you would have. Having excellent health and properly taking care of your body merely slows it down. The only way to stop it is not to be in it. It eats you up from inside. The only release from it is when you finally are able to extract yourself and your children from it as I can guarantee you that your children will have an idea of what is going on to. And they will not like seeing you go through it. It hurts and affects them whether you know it or not. Once they are older, children usually side with the parent that has repeatedly demonstrated they are all for them. They aren't stupid. They know whose really been taking care of them and looking out for their best interest. So for their sake, refer back to the beginning of this book and do not allow this sorry state to happen in the first place, if you can and it's not too late.